Bon Appétit

COOKING WITH
Bon Appétit

Pies and Tarts

THE KNAPP PRESS
Publishers
Los Angeles

Published by The Knapp Press
5900 Wilshire Boulevard, Los Angeles, California 90036

Library of Congress Cataloging in Publication Data

Main entry under title:

Pies and tarts.

  (Cooking with Bon appétit)
  Includes index.
  1. Pastry. I. Bon appétit. II. Series.
TX773.P534 1986   641.8'652   85-19722
ISBN 0-89535-173-0

On the cover: *Favorite Fresh Peach Pie*

Printed and bound in the United States of America

10   9   8   7   6   5

❦ Contents

❧ *Foreword*

Delicious, convenient and adaptable to every occasion, pies and tarts provide the perfect finishing touch to a meal, whether it's a casual family supper or a festive holiday dinner party. They can be homey and comforting, like a traditional deep-dish apple pie; or they can be showy dessert centerpieces, like a Chocolate Bavarian Hazelnut Torte. Plain or fancy, they are among America's favorite desserts.

The adaptable pie can be made with any number of fillings, whether they're fresh seasonal fruits or a creative mix of whatever happens to be on hand. A summer's harvest can provide the inspiration for a Lemon Curd and Fresh Blueberry Tart or Favorite Fresh Peach Pie. In winter, preserved fruits from the pantry and easy-to-find dairy products supply the ingredients for a warming Regal Raisin Date Pie or a creamy Buttermilk Custard Pie.

This collection of more than 200 recipes represents the best pies and tarts from the pages of *Bon Appétit*. Included are treasured family favorites, like Linda's Deep-Dish Apple Pie, Banana Cream Tarts, Tidewater Peanut Pie and Aunt Catfish's Boatsinker. There are a number of elegant desserts, from Crème Brûlée Tart Jimmy and Fresh Peach Tart to Hazelnut Custard Tart and Chocolate Mousse Pie with Raspberry Sauce. Busy cooks will love the convenience of frozen pies—Dark and White Chocolate Mousse Pie, Lemon Torte and Bountiful Hot Fudge Sundae Pie, to name just a few—that can be whisked from the freezer at a moment's notice.

A crisp, flaky pie crust or a pretty tart topped with a glistening mosaic of thinly sliced fruit is a triumph for any cook. Beginners as well as experienced bakers will appreciate the tips offered throughout this book. Suggestions for garnishes and serving ideas, for freezing crusts and baked pies, and an entire chapter devoted to creating the perfect crust make preparing these desserts almost as enjoyable as eating them.

1 ❦ Basic Crusts and Pastries

The crust is a pie's most vital "supporting character"—not the chief focus of attention, perhaps, but essential to overall success. When combined in proper proportion and with careful handling, simple ingredients are transformed into a golden, tender and flaky pastry—the first step toward a memorable dessert.

While the variations among different recipes produce endless nuances of flavor and texture, all pastry crusts share common ingredients: liquid, flour, fat, and a touch of salt to enhance flavor. The liquid, usually water or milk, binds the dough. Using too little liquid will result in a dry and crumbly pastry, but don't add any more than is needed to hold the dough together; too much liquid leads to toughness and shrinkage during baking. Be careful, too, to avoid handling the dough any more than necessary after the liquid is added, because this will toughen the pastry. All purpose flour is generally used in pie crusts, but we have also included a recipe for Whole Wheat Short Pastry (page 3) for those who prefer a tender crust with nutty whole-grain flavor.

Fat may be added in the form of butter, solid shortening or vegetable oil, alone or in combination. Butter gives rich flavor, crisp shortbread-like texture and a golden tint. Shortening makes a less flavorful but exceptionally flaky and well-textured crust, and vegetable oil makes for very tender pastry.

Throughout the book you will find tips and techniques to guide you to perfect pastrymaking. By following the recipes and keeping our suggestions in mind, your pie crusts will rival those of a professional baker—every time.

Pâte Brisée

Makes one 10-inch single crust

1⅓ cups bleached all purpose flour
½ cup (1 stick) well-chilled unsalted butter, cut into small pieces

½ teaspoon salt
2½ tablespoons (about) ice water

Blend first 3 ingredients in processor until coarse meal forms, using on/off turns. Add 2½ tablespoons water and process until dough just starts to gather together, adding more water if dough is dry and powdery; do not form ball. Transfer to plastic bag. Gently gather dough into ball. Flatten into disc. Refrigerate at least 45 minutes.

Can be prepared 1 day ahead.

Jody's Pie Crust

An easy crust made with vegetable oil.

Makes 1 unbaked 9-inch single crust

1 cup minus 1 tablespoon all purpose flour
¼ cup vegetable oil

2 tablespoons milk
Pinch of salt

Combine all ingredients in medium bowl and blend lightly. Gently form dough into ball. Roll dough out between sheets of waxed paper into 10-inch circle. Remove waxed paper, fold dough in half and then in half again. Transfer to pie plate. Unfold dough and fit into plate, trimming as necessary. Flute decoratively or press edge with fork.

Flaky Pastry

Makes 5 unbaked 9-inch single crusts

4 cups all purpose flour
1½ cups solid vegetable shortening
¼ cup (½ stick) butter
1 tablespoon sugar

1 tablespoon white vinegar
1 egg
½ cup water
2 teaspoons salt

Lightly grease five 9-inch pie plates. Combine flour, shortening, butter, sugar and vinegar in large bowl and blend with fingertips or fork until mixture resembles coarse meal. Beat egg in small bowl with water and salt. Add to flour mixture, tossing briefly with fork until just moistened. Divide into 5 equal portions. Gently form each into ball. Seal tightly with plastic wrap and chill at least 15 minutes. (*Dough can be prepared ahead to this point and frozen.*)

Generously flour work surface and rolling pin. Pat 1 portion of dough into circle and roll out. Turn dough over and flour again. Roll into 10-inch circle. Fold dough in half and then in half again. Transfer to pie plate. Unfold dough and fit into plate, leaving 1-inch overhang. Turn excess under to make narrow rolled rim. Flute decoratively or press edge with fork. Repeat with remaining portions of dough as needed.

❦ For Perfect Pastry

- The perfect flaky pastry is made of micro-thin alternating layers of flour and shortening. The way to achieve them is to have all ingredients chilled, so that the fat stays in tiny flakes rather than melting throughout the dough. Refrigerate all ingredients before starting and have the butter or shortening, in particular, very cold. Also chill the dough before rolling it out—an important step that relaxes the gluten in the flour and helps prevent stickiness. If possible, roll the dough on a marble slab or countertop that has been prechilled with a bag of ice.
- Work quickly and handle the dough as little as possible. The more it is worked the more gluten will develop, resulting in tough pastry.
- Overflouring the rolling surface will make the crust hard and dry. Use only as much flour as is absolutely necessary to prevent sticking—or try rolling out the dough between sheets of parchment or waxed paper.
- To transfer the rolled dough from work surface to pie pan, place the rolling pin on the edge of the pastry circle, roll the dough loosely over the pin and unroll it into the pan. Gently press it to uniform thickness, being careful not to stretch the dough. Trim the overhanging dough to an even one inch all around, then fold it in to form a double-thick edge before crimping.
- The best pie pans are those that absorb heat. Glass, dull aluminum and dark-finished metal are excellent; shiny metal pans, on the contrary, reflect heat and retard browning.
- Don't be tempted to remove the pie from the oven too soon just because the edges are browning rapidly. Simply cover them with a strip of foil and continue baking until the entire crust is golden brown.

Whole Wheat Short Pastry

Makes one 10- or 11-inch single crust or 36 to 48 hors d'oeuvre-size tartlet shells

2 cups whole wheat pastry flour
10 tablespoons (1¼ sticks) well-chilled unsalted butter, cut into ½-inch pieces
2 teaspoons fresh lemon juice
¼ to ⅓ cup ice water

Additional whole wheat pastry flour

Combine flour and butter in large bowl and blend with fingertips until mixture resembles coarse meal. Add lemon juice and ¼ cup ice water and blend well, working dough as little as possible and adding more water 1 tablespoon at a time if dough is too dry. Turn dough out onto unfloured work surface and quickly form into ball. Cover with plastic; chill 30 minutes.

Cut 2 pieces of waxed paper 24 inches long. Place 1 sheet on work surface and dust with additional flour. Set dough in center of paper and sprinkle with flour. Flatten dough with rolling pin and cover with remaining paper.

Roll dough out to thickness of ⅛ inch. Remove top sheet of waxed paper. Lifting bottom sheet, invert dough into 10- or 11-inch tart pan. Press dough firmly against sides and bottom. Run rolling pin over rim to trim off excess dough. Prick bottom and sides with fork (if filling to be used is liquid, such as custard, do not prick through).

Preheat oven to 350°F. Line pastry with waxed paper and fill with dried beans or rice. Bake 25 minutes. Discard paper and beans or rice. Continue baking until bottom is browned, about 10 minutes. Let cool. Fill as desired.

For tartlet shells: Arrange tartlet tins on baking sheet with sides touching. After rolling dough between sheets of waxed paper, remove top sheet. Lifting bottom sheet, invert dough over tins. Press dough firmly against sides and bottoms. Run rolling pin over top to trim off excess dough. Prick bottoms with fork. Line pastries with waxed paper and fill with dried beans or rice. Bake in 350°F oven 10 to 15 minutes, depending on size of tins. Discard paper and beans or rice. Continue baking until bottoms are browned, about 3 to 4 minutes.

Recipe will also make twelve 3½- to 4-inch tartlet shells.

Sweet Flaky Pie Crust

Because this pastry is very flaky, it requires partial baking before filling. For savory crust, use ½ teaspoon powdered sugar and ¼ teaspoon salt.

Makes one 9- or 10-inch single crust

1¼ cups pastry flour or all purpose flour
3 tablespoons powdered sugar
Pinch of salt

½ cup (1 stick) well-chilled unsalted butter, lard or margarine, cut into 10 pieces
4 to 5 tablespoons ice water

By hand: Combine flour, sugar and salt in large bowl and mix well. Cut in butter using pastry blender or 2 knives until mixture resembles coarse meal. Sprinkle 4 tablespoons water over mixture and, working quickly, squeeze into ball, adding remaining water if necessary. Turn dough out onto lightly floured surface and knead 2 or 3 times to blend. Pat into disc 1¼ inches thick. Flour lightly, wrap in plastic and refrigerate at least 1 hour or overnight.

In food processor: Combine flour, salt and sugar in processor and mix well. Add butter and blend using on/off turns until mixture is consistency of coarse meal. With machine running, add 4 tablespoons water through feed tube, mixing until flour is just moistened and starts to form dough; *stop machine before mixture forms ball or pie crust will be tough.* Turn out onto lightly floured surface and knead into ball. Complete crust according to directions above.

To form: Grease 9- or 10-inch pie pan or pie plate. Roll dough out on lightly floured surface into circle ⅛ inch thick. Ease dough into pan without stretching. Trim off excess but allow ½-inch overlap. Turn overlap under to make firm strong edge; flute decoratively. Refrigerate at least 1 hour.

To bake: Preheat oven to 425°F. Prick pie shell with fork. Line bottom of crust with greased foil or parchment paper and fill with dried beans or pie weights. For recipes that call for a lightly browned partially baked crust (such as custard pies), bake 20 minutes; discard foil and beans. Continue baking 7 minutes, then fill and bake as recipe specifies. For completely baked pie shell (for chiffon and other pies that do not require additional baking after filling), line as above and bake 20 minutes; discard foil and beans and continue baking until well browned, about 12 more minutes. Let cool completely before filling as desired.

❧ *Flours for Pastrymaking*

To assure moist, tender and delicate texture, pastry dough should be prepared with *soft winter wheat flours*. High in starch, these light flours quickly absorb fat, resulting in a minimum of mixing for rich baked goods. Unlike strong hard wheat flours, soft wheats produce minimal gluten, the protein that elasticizes pie crusts so they spring back when rolled out. Soft wheat is milled into both *cake flour* and *pastry flour*. When these are unavailable, *all purpose flour*, a blend of soft and hard wheat, can be substituted.

Pastry flour can be stone ground or roller-milled from the entire wheat kernel (*whole wheat pastry flour*) or it can be milled just from the heart of the kernel (*white pastry flour*). It is more granular than cake flour and forms more gluten, giving dough body so it doesn't tear or crumble as it is rolled out. Pastry dough must be worked to activate the gluten, but if it is overworked it will be tough and rubbery.

Cake flour is milled from the part of the wheat kernel that contains the most starch and, therefore, the least protein. It looks whiter and feels silkier and smoother than other flours; it often contains cornstarch.

Great Hints

- Check natural food stores when special flours cannot be found in local supermarkets.
- Flour can be pressed through a fine mesh sieve if sifter is not available.
- When substituting cake flour for an equivalent amount of all purpose flour, add 2 tablespoons *more* cake flour per cup. When substituting all purpose flour for cake flour, use 2 tablespoons *less*.
- Make your own low-gluten pastry flour from all purpose flour by substituting 1 tablespoon cornstarch for 1 tablespoon flour for every cup.
- Pie dough can be refrigerated up to 1 week. It will turn grayish if made from preservative-free unbleached flour, but its quality will not be affected.
- For a crisp brown crust when baking pies in porcelain or ceramic plates, place them on a heavy baking sheet that has been in the oven during preheating.

Buttery Pie Crust

Makes one 8- or 9-inch single crust

1½ cups all purpose flour, sifted
½ teaspoon salt
Pinch of sugar
6 tablespoons (¾ stick) butter

2 tablespoons plus 1 teaspoon solid vegetable shortening
4 to 5 tablespoons cold water

Combine flour, salt and sugar in large mixing bowl. Add butter and shortening in tablespoon-size pieces and cut into flour, using pastry blender or 2 knives, until mixture is size of small peas. Add water 1 tablespoon at a time and blend quickly with one hand, simultaneously gathering dough into a mass. Wrap with waxed paper and chill dough for at least 20 minutes.

When ready to bake, position rack in lower third of oven and preheat to 400°F. Flour work surface and rolling pin and roll dough into circle ⅛ inch thick. Fit into pie pan or flan ring; refrigerate about 15 minutes.

Line crust with foil and weight with dried beans, rice or pie weights. Bake 12 minutes. Discard foil and beans. Continue baking until bottom of pastry is lightly golden, about 5 minutes longer. Let crust cool completely before filling.

Magic Pie Crust

Makes 1 unbaked 9- or 10-inch single crust

1½ cups all purpose flour
¼ teaspoon salt
¾ cup solid vegetable shortening

1 egg
2 tablespoons cold water

Combine 1½ cups flour and salt in large bowl. Cut in shortening until mixture resembles coarse meal; do not overmix. Beat egg with water in small bowl. Add to flour mixture, tossing briefly with fork until just moistened. Gently form into ball. Generously flour work surface and rolling pin. Pat dough into circle and roll out. Turn dough over and flour again. Roll into 12-inch circle. Fold dough in half and then in half again. Transfer to pie plate. Unfold dough and fit into plate, trimming excess dough 1 inch beyond rim of pan. Turn excess under to make narrow rolled rim. Flute decoratively or crimp edge with fork.

Basic Pastry

Makes one 10-inch pie or tart crust

¾ cup (1½ sticks) well-chilled unsalted butter, cut into small pieces

1½ cups all purpose flour
2 tablespoons sugar
2 to 3 tablespoons ice water

Position rack in lower third of oven and preheat to 400°F. Place butter in processor work bowl. Add flour and sugar. With machine running, gradually pour water through feed tube, adding only enough so dough holds together; do not let dough form ball. Remove dough and lightly press into ball with hands. Flatten into disc.

Roll dough out on lightly floured surface to thickness of ⅛ inch. Fit into 10-inch metal quiche or flan pan; trim and flute edges. Line pastry with waxed paper and fill with dried beans, rice or pie weights. Bake 10 minutes. Reduce oven temperature to 375°F and bake 10 more minutes. Remove waxed paper and weights and return pie shell to oven for 3 to 5 more minutes. Remove from oven and fill as desired. Continue baking according to filling recipe.

2 🍎 *Fruit Pies*

From fresh peach pie served outdoors on a summer day to warm apple pie by a winter fireplace, fruit pies and tarts are a year-round treat. This collection includes recipes for every season and menu, showcasing old-fashioned favorites, impressive special-occasion desserts and lots of intriguing new flavor combinations.

Probably the best loved of all, apple pie never wanes in popularity—perhaps because there are so many variations that it is impossible to tire of them. To satisfy even the most determined traditionalist, try Linda's Deep-Dish Apple Pie (page 8) or Old World Apple Pie (page 10). Then there are apple recipes with a new twist—among them Swedish Apple Tart enriched with almond paste (page 11), Apple-Ginger Layered Tart in phyllo (page 13), and unusual Peppered Apple-Cheese Tart (page 19). As for other heritage fruit pies, few will be able to resist such classics as Glazed Strawberry Pie (page 35), Favorite Fresh Peach Pie (page 44), Deep-Dish Plum Pie (page 48), and Winter Fruit Pie (page 52).

Special dinners deserve a special touch, and this chapter includes a selection of desserts to round out a festive meal in style. Sour Cherry and Marzipan Tart (page 24), The Great Grape-Date Tart (page 26), Crème Brûlée Tart Jimmy (page 27), and Cookie Crust Tart with Boysenberry Puree (page 30) are terrific do-ahead treats that are sure to be a hit at any party. For an intimate dinner for two, try Raspberry-filled Meringue Tarts (page 35) or Rhubarb Tarts in Walnut Pastry (page 41). And for distinctive new flavor combinations, you might try Cherimoya, Strawberry and Kiwi Tart with Macadamia Nuts (page 39)—a delicate blend of fresh fruits, crisp *torten,* and passion fruit puree—or Tomato-Orange Tart (page 49), a unique Sicilian pastry featuring tomato preserves, pistachios and orange slices in a Marsala-enhanced crust.

Tightly sealed in freezer wrap, most unbaked fruit pies can be frozen up to four months; without thawing, bake at 425°F for 15 minutes, then at 350°F until done. Freezing lets you take advantage of the best seasonal produce, and in the depths of winter there are few delicacies to match a freshly baked pie bursting with ripe summer fruit.

❦ *Fresh Fruit*

Linda's Deep-Dish Apple Pie

6 to 8 servings

6 medium Granny Smith apples,
   peeled, cored and sliced
1 cup golden raisins
1/2 cup firmly packed light
   brown sugar
2 tablespoons all purpose flour
2 tablespoons water
2 tablespoons applejack
1 teaspoon cinnamon
1/2 cup chopped pecans

Brown Sugar Topping
1 1/2 cups firmly packed light
   brown sugar
1 cup all purpose flour
1/2 cup (1 stick) butter

Preheat oven to 350°F. Butter 9 1/2-inch deep-dish pan. Toss apples, raisins, brown sugar, flour, water, applejack and cinnamon in large bowl. Spoon into prepared pan. Sprinkle with chopped pecans.

For topping: Blend brown sugar, flour and butter until crumbly. Sprinkle evenly over apples. Bake until pie is brown and bubbly, about 50 minutes. Serve warm or at room temperature.

Apple Torte

10 to 12 servings

Crust
1 cup sifted all purpose flour
2 tablespoons sugar
1/4 teaspoon salt
1/2 cup (1 stick) butter
1 tablespoon vinegar

Filling
1 21-ounce can apple pie filling
2 to 3 apples, peeled, cored
   and diced

1/2 cup sugar
2 tablespoons all purpose flour
Juice of 1/2 lemon
1/2 teaspoon cinnamon
Whipped cream

For crust: Grease bottom and sides of 9-inch springform pan. Combine flour, sugar and salt in medium bowl. Cut in butter using pastry blender until mixture resembles coarse meal. Blend in vinegar. Press dough evenly onto bottom and sides of pan.

For filling: Preheat oven to 375°F. Combine all remaining ingredients except whipped cream in large bowl and blend well. Spoon into crust. Bake until top is golden, about 45 minutes. Let cool 5 minutes, then remove springform. Garnish each serving with dollop of whipped cream.

❦

🍏 *Hints for Freezing*

- Unbaked pie crust dough can be wrapped well and frozen for several months—in a ball shape, flattened into a disc or rolled out. A ball of dough large enough for a standard crust will take about three hours to thaw at room temperature; a rolled-out circle, 15 minutes.
- Baked or unbaked pie shells can also be frozen. If baked, they should be thoroughly cooled before wrapping and freezing.

  To defrost baked pie shells: Unwrap and thaw at room temperature for 15 minutes or in preheated 350°F oven for 8 minutes. The oven method is preferable, as it serves to recrisp the crust and freshen flavor.

  To bake frozen unbaked shells: Unwrap and place frozen shell in pre-heated 475°F oven until golden brown, about 8 to 10 minutes.
- Filled pies can be frozen, preferably prebaked (the crusts of unbaked pies tend to become soggy). Two-crust pies generally give better results than those with a single crust. Be sure to cool the baked pie thoroughly before wrapping and freezing.

  To defrost baked pies: Let pie stand at room temperature for 30 minutes, still wrapped. Unwrap and place in preheated 350°F oven about 30 minutes. Let cool 15 minutes before serving.

Streusel-topped Sour Cream Apple Pie

6 to 8 servings

¾ cup sugar
2 tablespoons all purpose flour
⅛ teaspoon salt
1 cup sour cream
1 egg
1 teaspoon vanilla
¼ teaspoon freshly grated nutmeg
1 20-ounce can sliced apples, partially drained
1 unbaked 9-inch deep-dish pie shell

Streusel Topping
⅓ cup sugar
⅓ cup all purpose flour
1 teaspoon cinnamon
¼ cup (½ stick) butter, cut into small pieces

Preheat oven to 400°F. Sift sugar, flour and salt into large bowl. Add sour cream, egg, vanilla and nutmeg and beat until smooth. Stir in apples. Pour mixture into pie shell. Bake 15 minutes. Reduce oven temperature to 350°F and continue baking until set, about 30 minutes.

For topping: Combine ingredients in medium bowl. Sprinkle evenly over pie. Increase oven temperature to 400°F. Bake until top is browned, about 10 minutes. Cool pie slightly before serving.

🍏

Old World Apple Pie

8 servings

1½ cups all purpose flour
6 tablespoons (¾ stick) well-chilled unsalted butter, cut into ¼-inch pieces
2 tablespoons well-chilled solid vegetable shortening
¼ teaspoon salt
3 to 4 tablespoons ice water

2½ pounds Rome Beauty apples, peeled, cored and sliced

2 cups firmly packed brown sugar
¼ cup cornstarch
3 tablespoons dark rum
1 teaspoon cinnamon
¾ cup chopped pecans
½ cup rolled oats
½ cup all purpose flour
½ cup (1 stick) butter, melted

Preheat oven to 350°F. Combine flour, butter, shortening and salt in chilled large bowl and blend until mixture resembles coarse meal. Add 3 tablespoons ice water and mix just until dough holds together, adding another tablespoon water if necessary. Form dough into ball; flatten into disc. Transfer to floured surface and roll out into 12-inch circle. Fit into 9-inch deep-dish pie pan, trimming excess. Prick bottom and sides of crust with fork. Bake 10 minutes. Retain oven temperature at 350°F.

Combine apples, 1 cup brown sugar, cornstarch, rum and cinnamon in large bowl and mix well. Spoon into pie shell. Combine remaining 1 cup brown sugar, pecans, oats, flour and melted butter in large bowl and mix well (*mixture will be crumbly.*) Sprinkle over apple mixture. Bake until top is golden brown and juices are bubbling, about 50 minutes. Serve pie warm.

Apple-Walnut Torte

6 to 8 servings

1 unbaked 9-inch pie crust

1 cup water
1½ cups sugar
4 large tart green apples, peeled, cored and coarsely chopped (about 3 cups)
1 vanilla bean, split lengthwise

¼ cup (½ stick) butter, room temperature
1 egg
1 cup finely ground walnuts
Whipped cream or ice cream

Preheat oven to 350°F. Prick pie shell with fork. Bake 10 minutes. Set aside to cool. Retain oven temperature at 350°F.

Combine water and 1 cup sugar in medium saucepan. Add apples and vanilla bean and bring to boil. Reduce heat to medium-low and simmer 5 minutes. Remove from heat and drain apples well; remove vanilla bean. Cream butter and remaining ½ cup sugar in medium bowl. Add egg and beat until fluffy. Blend in nuts. Arrange apples in pie shell. Spoon walnut mixture evenly over apples. Bake until crust is golden brown, about 40 minutes. Serve warm with whipped cream or ice cream.

Swedish Apple Tart

8 to 10 servings

Pastry
1½ cups all purpose flour
2 teaspoons sugar
½ teaspoon salt
½ cup well-chilled solid vegetable shortening, cut into small pieces
¼ cup (½ stick) well-chilled butter, cut into small pieces
Ice water

Almond-Hazelnut Frangipane
½ cup almond paste, room temperature
7 tablespoons sugar
2 extra-large eggs, room temperature
¼ cup (½ stick) butter, room temperature
¼ cup solid vegetable shortening, room temperature
¼ cup bread flour
¼ cup ground husked hazelnuts
½ teaspoon finely grated lemon peel

Apple Filling
3 cups peeled, cored and chopped tart green apple
¾ cup raisins
½ cup chopped walnuts
3 tablespoons sugar
1 teaspoon cinnamon
¼ teaspoon ground mace
⅛ teaspoon freshly grated nutmeg

Additional chopped walnuts
¼ cup powdered sugar beaten with 1½ teaspoons rum (glaze)

For pastry: Combine flour, sugar and salt in large bowl. Cut in shortening and butter with pastry blender or 2 knives until mixture resembles coarse meal. Blend in ice water until dough just comes together. Gather into ball and wrap in plastic. Refrigerate dough at least 30 minutes.

Roll dough out on lightly floured surface to thickness of ⅛ to ¼ inch. Fit into 11-inch tart pan; trim edges. Chill 30 minutes.

For frangipane: Beat almond paste and sugar in large bowl of electric mixer at low speed until well blended. Add eggs one at a time, beating well after each addition. Beat 5 minutes at medium speed. Cream butter and shortening in another bowl of electric mixer at high speed 5 minutes. Blend into almond paste mixture. Mix in flour, hazelnuts and finely grated lemon peel.

For filling: Combine apple, raisins, ½ cup walnuts, sugar, cinnamon, mace and nutmeg. Spread in bottom of pastry shell.

To assemble: Preheat oven to 350°F. Spoon frangipane into pastry bag fitted with plain tip. Pipe over apple filling; do not cover edges of pastry. Sprinkle with chopped walnuts. Bake until frangipane is set and pastry is lightly browned, about 1½ hours (if top browns too quickly, cover loosely with foil). Cool completely. Brush tart with glaze and serve.

Natural Apple Tart

10 servings

Pastry
- 3 cups all purpose flour
- 1/2 cup (1 stick) well-chilled butter
- 1/2 cup well-chilled vegetable shortening
- 1/2 teaspoon salt
- 1/2 cup ice water

Glaze
- 1 1/2 cups peeled coarsely chopped Delicious apple
- 1 1/2 cups thawed frozen apple juice concentrate

Filling
- 3 tablespoons thawed frozen apple juice concentrate

- 9 cups paper-thin peeled apple slices

- Cinnamon
- 2 tablespoons fresh lemon or lime juice or to taste

- 1/3 cup toasted unsweetened shredded coconut
- Sour cream or plain yogurt (optional)

For pastry: Generously grease bottom and sides of large baking sheet. Combine flour, butter, shortening and salt in large bowl and blend until mixture is crumbly and size of small peas. Add water and mix until dough comes clean from bowl. Place dough in plastic bag, shape into ball, then flatten into disc. Refrigerate for at least 30 minutes.

Preheat oven to 375°F. Roll dough out paper-thin on floured work surface. Fit into baking sheet, turning up at edge to form lip. Bake until pastry just begins to color, about 15 minutes. Let cool.

For glaze: Combine apple and concentrate in saucepan and simmer, stirring frequently, until thick. Transfer to processor or blender and puree until smooth. Return to saucepan.

For filling: Heat 1 tablespoon concentrate in large nonstick skillet over medium-low heat. Add 3 cups apple slices and sauté until softened. Remove with slotted soon. Repeat twice.

To assemble: Spread filling over pastry and sprinkle with cinnamon and lemon juice (for tarter flavor). Bake until pastry is golden and apples are cooked but not mushy, about 20 to 25 minutes.

Add coconut to glaze and reheat, stirring constantly. Spread over apples. Cool to room temperature before slicing into squares. Serve with dollop of sour cream or yogurt if desired.

Royal Dutch Treat

Makes 24 small tartlets

- 1 cup (2 sticks) unsalted butter, room temperature
- 2 cups firmly packed turbinado or brown sugar
- 2 cups unbleached all purpose flour

- 6 small Pippin or Greening apples, peeled, cored and cut into 1/4-inch slices
- Turbinado or brown sugar
- Cinnamon

Combine butter, 2 cups brown sugar and flour in large bowl and mix with fingertips until mixture resembles coarse meal, about 10 minutes. Knead until dough forms ball. Cover with plastic wrap and seal tightly. Refrigerate dough 4 to 5 hours or overnight.

Let dough stand at room temperature 30 minutes. Meanwhile, grease and flour 24 2½- to 3-inch tartlet pans with removable bottoms. Arrange pans on baking sheet. Pinch off 2 to 3 tablespoons of dough and roll into ball. Press into bottom and evenly up sides of tartlet pan. Repeat with remaining dough. Arrange 4 to 6 apple slices in each. Dust each lightly with brown sugar and cinnamon.

Preheat oven to 350°F. Bake tartlets until light brown and crisp, about 25 to 30 minutes. Let cool slightly before removing from baking pans.

Caramelized Apples on Puff Pastry (La Tarte Tatin)

4 servings

8 ounces puff pastry (fresh or thawed frozen)

½ cup sugar
¼ cup water
5 pounds Golden Delicious apples, peeled, cored, quartered and tossed with fresh lemon juice

½ cup sugar
½ teaspoon cinnamon
¼ cup (½ stick) unsalted butter, melted

Sugar

For pastry: Preheat oven to 300°F. Roll pastry ⅛ inch thick. Cut into circle 1 inch larger than diameter of 1-quart soufflé dish. Transfer to baking sheet, prick with a fork and bake 30 minutes; if not quite browned, increase heat to 350°F and continue baking until golden brown. Let cool on wire rack.

Preheat oven to 350°F. Combine ½ cup sugar with water in 8-inch skillet and cook, swirling pan frequently, until mahogany colored. Pour into 1-quart soufflé dish. Begin adding apples, arranging vertically (fill dish as compactly as possible since fruit will shrink during baking). Lay remaining apples (or as many as possible) on top.

Sprinkle with remaining ½ cup sugar and cinnamon. Pour melted butter evenly over top. Cover with foil, making several slits to allow steam to escape. Lay piece of foil on lower oven rack to catch any juices that might overflow. Bake, basting frequently, until apples are tender, about 1½ hours. Remove from oven and cool 15 minutes. Carefully pour off juices into 8-inch skillet and boil over medium-high heat until reduced and caramelized.

Run knife around inside of soufflé dish to loosen apples. Set pastry over fruit. Place serving plate on top and invert. Pour caramelized juices over top. Heat heavy skillet until quite hot. Dust tarte with sugar and hold bottom of hot skillet over top of tarte to sear sugar, or place under broiler. Repeat 3 more times. Serve warm or at room temperature.

Apple-Ginger Layered Tart

8 servings

2 cups water
1 cup sugar
3 slices crystallized ginger, cut into thin strips
¼ cup dried currants
1 tablespoon unsalted butter
Pinch of salt
8 tart apples (3½ to 3¾ pounds total), peeled, cored, quartered and cut into ⅛-inch slices

½ cup walnuts
½ cup fine dry breadcrumbs

6 sheets phyllo pastry
⅓ cup (about) unsalted butter, melted

Sugar
Whipping cream (optional)

Combine water and 1 cup sugar in large skillet and bring to boil over medium-high heat, stirring until sugar is dissolved. Add ginger and let boil 5 minutes *without stirring.* Remove from heat. Add currants, 1 tablespoon butter and salt. Add apple slices and toss lightly. Return to medium-high heat, cover and bring to boil. Let mixture boil 5 minutes.

Turn apple slices over and continue boiling, uncovered, until liquid is almost evaporated, turning apples occasionally, about 15 minutes. Reduce heat and simmer gently until apples are tender, about 5 minutes. Transfer apples to bowl using slotted spoon. Boil any liquid remaining in pan until reduced and thickened. Pour over apples and toss gently. Set aside to cool.

Meanwhile, preheat oven to 350°F. Arrange walnuts on baking sheet. Bake until lightly toasted, about 10 minutes. Let cool. Chop walnuts finely. Transfer to small bowl. Add breadcrumbs and blend well.

To assemble: Lay phyllo pastry on sheet of plastic wrap and cover with another piece of plastic. Set third plastic sheet on work surface and lay 1 phyllo sheet on it, re-covering remainder with plastic to prevent drying. Brush phyllo sheet with melted butter and sprinkle with some of nut mixture. Set another sheet of phyllo directly over first. Brush with melted butter and sprinkle with some of nut mixture. Drape phyllo sheets over rolling pin. Transfer to 7½- to 8-inch springform pan buttered side up, easing gently, fitting into pan and letting phyllo overlap sides.

Lay another sheet of phyllo on damp towel. Using saucepan lid or plate about same size diameter as springform, cut 2 circles from phyllo using tip of sharp knife or scissors. Brush circles with melted butter and sprinkle with some of nut mixture. Stack buttered side up in bottom of springform pan, using rolling pin if necessary.

Spoon ⅓ of apple mixture into pan. Sprinkle with some of nut mixture. Cut 2 more circles from another sheet of phyllo. Brush with melted butter and sprinkle with some of nut mixture. Arrange buttered side up over apples. Spoon another ⅓ of apples into pan. Sprinkle with some of nuts. Cut 2 more circles from another sheet of phyllo. Brush with melted butter and sprinkle with some of nut mixture. Arrange buttered side up over apples. Top phyllo with remaining apples. Sprinkle with some of nut mixture. Fold overlap up to cover filling. Brush top with melted butter. Cut 2 circles from remaining sheet of phyllo. Brush with melted butter and sprinkle with nut mixture. Set phyllo on top of tart.

Preheat oven to 350°F. Remove sides of springform. Place sheet of aluminum foil, shiny side down, over top of tart. Gently pinch foil around sides of tart. Carefully turn tart over (using your hand to support it) and transfer to heavy baking sheet (do not remove foil). Remove bottom of springform. Flatten out foil. Brush melted butter over tart. Bake 45 minutes.

Preheat broiler. Sprinkle top of tart with sugar. Broil until sugar is caramelized and top is golden, watching carefully to prevent burning, about 1 minute. Serve warm or at room temperature. Pass cream separately.

Special Apple Pie

8 servings

Crust
1³/₄ cups all purpose flour
¹/₄ cup sugar
 1 teaspoon cinnamon
¹/₂ teaspoon salt
10 tablespoons (1¹/₄ sticks) butter
¹/₄ cup water or apple cider

Filling
 8 McIntosh apples, peeled, cored
   and sliced
1²/₃ cups sour cream
 1 cup sugar
¹/₃ cup all purpose flour

 1 egg
 2 teaspoons vanilla
¹/₂ teaspoon salt

Topping
 1 cup chopped walnuts
¹/₂ cup all purpose flour
¹/₃ cup firmly packed brown sugar
¹/₃ cup granulated sugar
 1 tablespoon cinnamon
   Pinch of salt
¹/₂ cup (1 stick) butter,
   room temperature

For crust: Combine flour, sugar, cinnamon and salt in medium bowl. Cut in butter using pastry blender or 2 knives until mixture resembles coarse meal. Add water and toss mixture gently with fork until evenly moistened. Gather gently into ball. Transfer to lightly floured board and roll into circle slightly larger than deep 10-inch pie plate. Ease pastry into pan and flute a high edge. Set aside.

For filling: Preheat oven to 450°F. Combine apples, sour cream, sugar, flour, egg, vanilla and salt in large bowl and mix well. Spoon into crust. Bake 10 minutes. Reduce oven temperature to 350°F and continue baking until filling is slightly puffed and golden brown, about 40 minutes. (If edges of crust begin to brown too quickly, cover with strips of aluminum foil.)

For topping: Meanwhile, combine walnuts, flour, sugars, cinnamon and salt in medium bowl and mix well. Blend in butter until mixture is crumbly. Spoon over pie and bake 15 minutes longer. Serve warm or at room temperature.

Cranberry and Apple Pie

Vanilla ice cream is a nice accompaniment to this tart winter fruit dessert from Aux Anciens Canadiens, a celebrated Montréal restaurant.

6 to 8 servings

 Dough for 9-inch
 double-crust pie
 2 cups cranberries
 4 medium tart green apples, peeled,
   cored and sliced ¹/₈ inch thick

 1 cup sugar*
 2 tablespoons all purpose flour
 1 teaspoon freshly grated nutmeg

Preheat oven to 450°F. Roll dough out on lightly floured surface to thickness of ¹/₈ inch. Cut out two 11-inch rounds. Fit 1 round into 9-inch pie plate. Combine cranberries, apples, sugar, flour and nutmeg. Spoon into pie plate. Cover with second round. Seal edges; crimp decoratively. Make slits in top to allow steam to escape. Bake 10 minutes. Reduce oven temperature to 375°F. Bake until crust is golden brown and fruit is tender, 35 to 40 minutes. Serve warm or chilled.

*Add up to ½ cup more sugar if sweeter filling is desired.

Deep-Dish Apple-Bourbon Pie

We've given this American classic a few new twists that make it wonderfully spicy and crunchy.

6 to 8 servings

7 large Granny Smith or Pippin apples, peeled, cored and sliced
1 cup coarsely chopped walnuts, toasted
¾ cup raisins
½ cup plus 2 tablespoons firmly packed dark brown sugar
2 tablespoons all purpose flour
2 tablespoons bourbon
1½ tablespoons butter, room temperature

½ to ¾ teaspoon allspice
½ to ¾ teaspoon cinnamon
¼ teaspoon ground ginger
Juice of 1 lemon
Pinch of salt
Pinch of ground cloves

Sweet Rough Puff Pastry with walnuts*
1 egg, beaten (optional)

Position rack in center of oven and preheat to 400°F. Grease 6- to 7-cup soufflé or deep pie dish. Combine all ingredients except pastry and egg and blend well. Turn into prepared dish. Roll out pastry to thickness of about ⅛ inch. Place over filling. Trim to fit top of dish and seal against rim. Brush pastry with egg, if desired. Roll out remaining pastry and use for decoration; brush again with egg. Bake until crust is golden brown and juices are bubbly, about 45 minutes. (If top browns too quickly, cover loosely with foil.) Serve warm or at room temperature.

*Sweet Rough Puff Pastry with Nuts

1 cup unbleached all purpose flour
⅓ cup ground walnuts (filberts, almonds, macadamia nuts or cashews may be substituted)
¼ cup cake flour
1 tablespoon sugar
1 teaspoon allspice (optional but delicious with apple pie)

6 tablespoons (¾ stick) well-chilled unsalted butter
¼ cup cold water
3 tablespoons unsalted butter, softened

Combine dry ingredients and mix in large bowl. Cut in butter with pastry blender until coarse meal forms. Add water, tossing with a fork until dough is just moistened and can be gathered into a loose ball. Wrap dough in waxed paper and refrigerate 30 minutes. Have 3 tablespoons softened butter ready.

Roll pastry into 9 × 18-inch rectangle. Spread ⅔ of pastry with 1 tablespoon butter. Fold unbuttered third over half of buttered area. Fold remaining third over top of pastry (as if folding a business letter). Turn pastry to open as you would a book and roll again into rectangle. Spread ⅔ of pastry with 2 tablespoons remaining butter. Fold as before, wrap and chill about 45 minutes (or up to 2 days). Repeat rolling, folding and turning process two more times. Wrap and chill in refrigerator from 2 to 24 hours. (*Pastry can be frozen at this point or refrigerated up to 4 days.*)

Swiss Apple Tart

4 to 6 serving

Crust

1¼ cups all purpose flour
  5 tablespoons sugar
    Pinch of salt
  6 tablespoons (¾ stick) butter,
    well chilled
2½ tablespoons shortening,
    well chilled
  1 egg yolk
  3 to 4 tablespoons pear brandy

Filling

  3 to 4 tart, firm apples, peeled,
    cored and sliced
    about ¼ inch thick
    Juice of 1 lemon
  ⅓ to ½ cup sugar
21 tablespoons (¼ stick) butter

    Crème Anglaise*

For crust: Combine flour, sugar and salt in medium bowl and mix well. Cut in butter and shortening until mixture resembles coarse meal. Using a fork, toss in egg yolk and 3 tablespoons brandy; *do not stir or beat mixture.* If dough cannot be gathered into ball, toss in another tablespoon brandy. *Do not overwork.* As soon as dough can be gathered into ball, wrap and refrigerate overnight. (*Can be stored in refrigerator 2 to 3 days.*)

When ready to complete tart, grease 8-inch tart pan with removable bottom. Roll dough ⅛ inch thick and fit carefully into pan. Refrigerate 30 minutes.

Preheat oven to 400°F. Remove crust from refrigerator and line with foil. Fill with dried beans or rice. Bake 10 minutes; remove foil and beans and continue baking an additional 5 minutes, or until crust just begins to turn golden. Remove from oven and allow to cool on rack in pan.

For filling: While crust cools, toss apples with lemon juice and half of sugar. Arrange in crust in tightly packed spiral or circular pattern. Place on baking sheet and bake 20 minutes, or until apples are almost tender. Sprinkle with remaining sugar and dot with butter. Continue baking another 10 minutes. Remove from oven and cool on rack. Serve at room temperature or slightly warm with Crème Anglaise spooned over each slice. (*Tart may be reheated in slow oven.*)

*Crème Anglaise

Makes about 2½ cups

2 cups half and half
4 egg yolks, room temperature
½ cup sugar

½ vanilla bean, split in
  half lengthwise

Chill medium mixing bowl. Place half and half in heavy-bottomed, nonaluminum saucepan over medium heat and bring to just below boiling. Beat together yolks and sugar until mixture is pale yellow. Pour a little hot half and half into yolk mixture and mix gently. Return mixture to saucepan and add vanilla bean.

Cook over medium-low heat, stirring constantly with whisk, until mixture coats spoon, about 8 to 10 minutes. *Do not boil or mixture will curdle.* Remove from heat, transfer to chilled bowl and stir constantly until custard is room temperature. Remove vanilla bean. Cover and chill until ready to serve.

Country Apple Tart

This rustic-looking dessert has a yeast dough crust with a hint of lemon.

12 servings

1 envelope dry yeast
1 cup lukewarm milk
(80°F to 90°F)
4½ cups plus 2 tablespoons
unbleached all purpose flour

¼ cup (½ stick) butter
¼ cup sugar
1 egg
1 tablespoon grated lemon peel
½ teaspoon salt

¼ cup (½ stick) butter, melted
½ cup fresh breadcrumbs

4 pounds Delicious apples,
peeled, cored and cut
into ½-inch wedges
½ cup dried currants or raisins,
soaked in ⅓ cup brandy
and drained
½ cup almond slivers
Sugar
1 cup whipping cream whipped
with 1 teaspoon vanilla

Dissolve yeast in half of milk. Sift flour into large bowl. Make well in center. Pour yeast mixture into well. Gradually stir in enough flour from sides of well to form spongelike mixture in well. Sprinkle top of "sponge" with flour. Let rest in warm area until top of sponge appears taut and slightly stretched, for about 15 minutes.

Melt ¼ cup butter in remaining milk. Using wooden spoon, mix ¼ cup sugar, egg, lemon peel, salt and butter mixture into sponge mixture, incorporating flour from around sponge, until dough is smooth and does not stick to bowl.

Turn dough out onto lightly floured surface. Knead until smooth and elastic. Return dough to bowl. Let rise in warm draft-free area until doubled in volume, about 1½ hours.

Punch dough down. Turn out onto lightly floured surface and knead several times. Roll dough out to same size as shallow baking pan (about 1½ x 12 × 17 inches). Grease pan. Transfer dough to pan; roll edges to form rim. Let dough rise about 10 minutes.

Position rack at lowest setting in oven and preheat to 375°F. Brush surface of dough with melted butter. Sprinkle with breadcrumbs. Arrange apple slices upright over dough in lengthwise rows. Sprinkle raisins and almonds evenly between rows. Bake until crust pulls away from sides of pan and top is lightly browned, about 1¼ hours. Transfer to upper rack; increase oven temperature to 400°F. Bake until browned and crusty, about 15 minutes. Sprinkle generously with sugar. Serve warm or at room temperature. Pass whipped cream separately.

Open-Face Apple Coconut Pie

6 to 8 servings

3 medium-size tart green apples,
peeled, cored and sliced ¼ inch
thick (about 4 cups)
1 unbaked 9-inch pie crust
1 cup sugar
⅓ teaspoon cinnamon
2 tablespoons (¼ stick) butter, cut
into ½-inch pieces

2 cups flaked coconut
½ cup evaporated milk
1 egg, beaten to blend
Ice cream

Preheat oven to 425°F. Arrange apples in single layer in pie shell. Combine ½ cup sugar with cinnamon in small bowl and sprinkle over apples. Dot with butter. Bake until crust is golden, 25 minutes.

Meanwhile, combine coconut, milk, egg and remaining ½ cup sugar in medium bowl and beat well. Pour over apple mixture. Reduce oven temperature to 325°F and continue baking until coconut is toasted, about 20 minutes. Serve at room temperature with ice cream.

Peppered Apple-Cheese Tart

This unusual dessert is best served the day it is prepared.

8 to 10 servings

Pastry
1½ cups sifted all purpose flour
¼ cup sugar
½ teaspoon salt
Pinch of freshly ground black pepper
½ cup (1 stick) plus 1 tablespoon well-chilled butter, cut into 1½-inch pieces
1 egg, beaten to blend

Apple Filling
½ cup (1 stick) butter
6 apples, peeled, cored and cut into eighths
½ to ¾ cup sugar

Cheese Custard
2 eggs
⅓ cup grated caciocavallo cheese
¼ cup sugar
1 teaspoon all purpose flour
Pinch of salt
1 cup half and half

1 teaspoon coarsely cracked black pepper

For pastry: Blend sifted flour, sugar, salt and pepper on work surface. Cut in butter with fingertips until consistency of coarse meal. Make large well in center. Add beaten egg 1 tablespoon at a time, working in flour with fingers until dough just holds together (entire egg may not be necessary). Form dough into ball. With heel of hand, push dough in small pieces down onto surface away from you to blend butter and flour thoroughly. Repeat once. Gather dough into ball; flatten into disc. Wrap in plastic and refrigerate at least 1 hour.

Butter 9- to 10-inch porcelain quiche dish or pie plate. Roll dough out on lightly floured surface into circle ¹⁄₁₆ inch thick. Fit into pan; form edges. Prick with fork. Freeze until firm.

Preheat oven to 375°F. Line pastry with buttered parchment, then fill with dried beans or pie weights. Bake 5 minutes. Remove parchment and weights and bake 8 minutes. Cool while preparing apple filling.

For apple filling: Melt butter in heavy large skillet over medium-high heat. Stir in apple; sprinkle with sugar (amount will depend on sweetness of apples). Cook until well-caramelized but still firm, stirring occasionally, about 10 minutes. Remove slices with slotted spoon. Cool on plate. Remove skillet from heat and pour off excess butter. Set skillet aside.

For custard: Mix eggs with cheese, sugar, flour and salt in large bowl. Blend in half and half. Adjust seasoning. Stir into same skillet, scraping up any browned bits clinging to bottom.

To assemble: Preheat oven to 375°F. Arrange apples in crust. Bake 30 minutes. Pour custard over. Sprinkle with coarsely cracked pepper. Continue baking until set, about 20 minutes. Serve warm or at room temperature.

Apple Pie with Chestnuts (Tarte Tatin aux Marrons)

*Make this in the fall
and winter months when
fresh chestnuts are
readily available.*

Makes one 10-inch pie

Pâte Brisée
1 cup unbleached all purpose flour
¼ teaspoon sugar
⅛ teaspoon salt
6 tablespoons (¾ stick) well-chilled unsalted butter, cut into ½-inch pieces
1 tablespoon white vinegar
1 tablespoon (about) cold water

⅔ cup sugar
½ cup water

10 to 12 whole chestnuts
3 tablespoons golden raisins
2 tablespoons Calvados

¼ cup (½ stick) unsalted butter
6 cups peeled, sliced cooking apples
3 tablespoons sugar
2 tablespoons chestnut puree*
1½ teaspoons grated lemon peel

1 egg, beaten to blend

For pâte brisée: Mix flour, sugar and salt in processor. Add butter and process using on/off turns until dough resembles coarse meal. With machine running, pour vinegar and water through feed tube and mix well; do not let dough form ball. Turn out onto work surface and pat into flat disc. Wrap in waxed paper and chill 30 minutes.

Combine ⅔ cup sugar and ½ cup water in small saucepan and cook over low heat until sugar is dissolved, swirling pan occasionally. Increase heat to medium-high and cook until mixture is caramel colored. Pour syrup evenly into 10-inch pie pan, tilting pan to partially coat sides. Set pan aside.

Peel ⅛-inch strip of shell from one side of each chestnut. Place chestnuts in medium saucepan and cover with cold water. Bring to boil over high heat and continue boiling 1 minute. Remove from heat. Discard water in saucepan. Peel shells and inner skins from chestnuts and discard. Return chestnuts to same saucepan and cover with cold water. Bring to boil over high heat. Reduce heat and simmer until chestnuts are tender when pierced with sharp knife, about 45 to 60 minutes. Drain well. Cut chestnuts into thirds and transfer to small bowl. Add raisins and Calvados. Set mixture aside.

Melt ¼ cup butter in large skillet over medium heat. Add apple slices, sugar, chestnut puree and lemon peel and sauté until apples are almost tender, 3 to 5 minutes, being careful not to break apple slices. Transfer mixture to large baking sheet and let stand until cool enough to handle. Arrange apple slices in prepared pie pan in overlapping circles from middle of pan out to edge. (Pie will be inverted so nicest slices should be on bottom.) Fill center with remaining apples. Top with chestnut mixture.

Preheat oven to 400°F. Roll dough out between 2 sheets of waxed paper into 11-inch circle. Invert dough circle over apple slices, folding under edge, trimming off excess and sealing slightly above rim of pan. Brush top of dough with beaten egg and prick with fork. Transfer pie to baking sheet. Bake until golden brown, about 45 minutes. Run knife around edge of crust to loosen. Cool pie 5 minutes. Place serving platter over top of pie and quickly invert onto plate. Let cool slightly and serve warm.

*If chestnut puree is unavailable, substitute 2 tablespoons additional sugar.

Apple-Pecan Upside-Down Pie

8 servings

Crust
- 3 cups all purpose flour, sifted
- 1 teaspoon salt
- ³/4 cup (1¹/2 sticks) butter
- 6 tablespoons (about) ice water

Topping
- ³/4 cup chopped pecans (about 3 ounces)
- ¹/2 cup firmly packed light brown sugar
- ¹/4 cup (¹/2 stick) butter, melted

Filling
- ¹/2 cup sugar
- 3 tablespoons all purpose flour
- 2 tablespoons cinnamon
- Pinch of salt
- Pinch of freshly grated nutmeg
- ¹/4 cup (¹/2 stick) butter, melted
- 4 large tart green apples (about 2 pounds), peeled, cored and cut into 1-inch chunks

For crust: Combine flour and salt in large bowl. Using pastry blender or 2 knives, cut in butter until mixture resembles coarse meal. Stir in enough water so dough comes together. Gather into ball. Wrap in plastic and refrigerate at least 1 hour or overnight.

Divide dough into 2 pieces, one slightly larger than the other. Roll each piece out on lightly floured surface to thickness of ³/16 inch.

For topping: Combine pecans and sugar in medium bowl. Add butter and stir until mixture is crumbly. Sprinkle over bottom of 10-inch deep-dish pie pan. Fit larger dough circle into pan, leaving 1 inch overhang.

For filling: Preheat oven to 350°F. Combine sugar, flour, cinnamon, salt and nutmeg in another large bowl. Stir in butter. Add apples and toss to coat thoroughly. Mound apples in prepared pan. Cover with smaller dough circle. Trim, seal and flute edges. Cut 4 vents in top to allow steam to escape. Bake pie until golden brown, about 1¹/4 hours.

Cool pie completely in pan. To remove, run knife around edge to loosen. Place pan on hot griddle 5 minutes to soften topping. Invert pie onto platter, removing pan slowly. Serve immediately.

Apricot-Apple Tart

8 servings

Sweet Crust
- 1³/4 cups all purpose flour
- 1 tablespoon sugar
- ¹/2 cup (1 stick) well-chilled unsalted butter, cut into 1-inch pieces
- 1 egg yolk
- 2 tablespoons water

Apricot-Apple Filling
- ¹/2 cup sugar
- 1¹/2 pounds Granny Smith apples, peeled, cored and cut into ¹/2-inch-wide slices

- 6 tablespoons (³/4 stick) butter
- 6 ounces dried apricot halves, soaked in warm water 20 minutes

- 3 tablespoons ground almonds
- 2 tablespoons sugar
- 1 egg, room temperature
- 1 egg yolk, room temperature
- ¹/2 cup whipping cream
- 1 tablespoon orange liqueur
- 2 tablespoons strained apricot jam, melted (optional)

For crust: Blend dry ingredients and butter in processor using on/off turns until mixture resembles coarse meal. Mix in yolk and water and blend until dough just begins to come together. Gather dough into ball, flatten into disc and wrap with plastic. Refrigerate at least 30 minutes. (*Can be prepared several days ahead and refrigerated.*)

Preheat oven to 400°F. Generously butter 11- or 12-inch tart pan with removable bottom. Roll dough out on lightly floured surface into 3/16-inch-thick round. Gently fit dough into prepared pan, trimming and finishing edges. Refrigerate at least 10 minutes.

Prick bottom crust with fork. Line with parchment. Fill with dried beans or rice. Bake 15 minutes. Remove beans and parchment. Bake until pastry shell is brown, about 8 minutes. Cool.

For filling: Spread ½ cup sugar on large plate. Coat apple slices with sugar, reserving remainder. Melt 3 tablespoons butter in heavy large skillet over high heat. Add apples when butter begins to brown and stir gently until sugar caramelizes and apples are golden brown, about 8 minutes. Cool on plate. Drain apricots and pat dry. Wash and dry skillet. Dip apricots in sugar and caramelize in remaining 3 tablespoons butter as for apples. Cool.

Preheat oven to 375°F. Mix almonds and 2 tablespoons sugar in small bowl. Stir in egg and yolk. Blend in cream and liqueur. Arrange fruit in alternate concentric circles in pastry shell. Pour filling over fruit. Bake until custard is set, about 20 minutes. Cool on rack 10 minutes. Brush jam over tart if desired. Serve tart warm.

Chef Dussaud's Summer Fruit Tart (Tarte aux Fruits d'Eté)

8 servings

1¼ cups all purpose flour, sifted
3 tablespoons sugar
½ teaspoon salt
½ cup (1 stick) well-chilled butter, cut into small pieces
1 egg

2 cups diced peeled apricot
½ cup diced peeled peach

½ cup diced peeled plum
½ cup diced orange
1 small banana, diced
3 eggs, room temperature
¾ cup whipping cream
¼ cup sugar
1 tablespoon finely grated lemon peel

Combine flour, sugar and salt in large bowl. Cut in butter until mixture resembles coarse meal. Mix in egg until dough just holds together. Gather into ball. Turn out onto work surface. With heel of hand, push small pieces of dough onto surface away from you to blend butter and flour thoroughly. Wrap in plastic and refrigerate 30 minutes.

Roll dough out on lightly floured surface into 13-inch circle about ⅛ inch thick. Fit into 11-inch tart pan with removable bottom. Trim and form edges. Prick bottom of shell with fork. Refrigerate at least 1 hour.

Preheat oven to 375°F. Set baking sheet in oven. Line bottom of tart shell with foil. Fill with pie weights or dried beans. Bake until set, about 20 minutes. Remove foil and weights. Bake crust until brown, about 10 minutes.

Sprinkle fruit into crust. Whisk eggs until blended. Stir in cream, sugar and peel. Pour over fruit. Set tart on preheated sheet. Bake until filling is set, about 30 minutes, covering edges with foil if crust browns too quickly. Cool tart to room temperature before serving.

Caramelized Fig Tart (Tarte aux Figues des Hautes Vallées)

8 servings

1½ cups sifted all purpose flour
1 tablespoon superfine sugar
½ teaspoon salt
½ teaspoon cinnamon
½ teaspoon finely grated lemon peel
9 tablespoons unsalted butter, cut into tablespoons, room temperature
1 egg, beaten to blend

Superfine sugar

24 canned Kadota figs

Whipped cream flavored with powdered sugar and finely grated lemon peel (optional)

Combine flour, sugar, salt, cinnamon and lemon peel in processor. Blend in 7 tablespoons butter using on/off turns until mixture resembles coarse meal. With machine running, add beaten egg through feed tube in slow steady stream, mixing just until dough comes together; do not form ball (entire egg may not be necessary). Flatten dough into disc ½ inch high. Wrap in waxed paper and chill at least 1 hour.

Coat 9- to 10-inch false-bottom tart pan with remaining 2 tablespoons butter. Sprinkle bottom and sides with sugar. Roll dough out on lightly floured surface to thickness of ⅙ inch. Fit into pan; trim and form edges. Refrigerate pastry shell 30 minutes.

Position rack in bottom of oven and preheat to 400°F. Drain figs thoroughly, reserving syrup. Pat figs dry; cut in half. Arrange halves seed side up in concentric circles in pastry shell. Bake 30 minutes. Remove tart from oven. Reposition rack in top of oven.

Cook syrup over high heat until reduced to ⅓ cup. Brush figs and rim of crust with syrup. Continue baking until figs and crust are caramelized, 15 to 20 minutes. Immediately remove tart from pan and slide carefully onto lightly buttered rack. Let cool. Serve with whipped cream if desired.

Miniature Cherry Tarts

Makes 12

2¼ cups sifted all purpose flour
1 teaspoon salt
¾ cup solid vegetable shortening
6 tablespoons ice water

1 16-ounce can tart cherries in water, drained (reserve liquid)
¾ cup sugar

2 tablespoons cornstarch
¼ teaspoon salt
2 tablespoons (¼ stick) butter
Whipped cream (optional)

Preheat oven to 400°F. Lightly butter *outside* of 12 muffin tin cups. Combine flour and salt in medium bowl. Cut in shortening using pastry blender or 2 knives until mixture resembles coarse meal. Set ⅔ of dough aside. Add ice water to remaining ⅓ and blend well. Return reserved dough to bowl and mix well. Gather pastry into ball. Roll out on lightly floured surface to thickness of ⅛ inch. Cut out 12 circles, using 3½-inch round cutter. Mold circles around outsides of prepared muffin cups. Prick pastry shells with fork. Bake until lightly browned, about 25 minutes. Cool crusts briefly on cups, then transfer to rack to cool.

Heat reserved liquid from cherries in medium saucepan over medium heat. Add sugar, cornstarch and salt. Cook just until thickened, clear and smooth, 4 to 5 minutes. Remove from heat. Add cherries and butter and mix well. Cool to room temperature. Spoon into crusts. Top each with whipped cream.

Sour Cherry and Marzipan Tart

Layers of tart-sweet fresh cherries and rich marzipan in a crisp almond cookie crust. (Pitted sour cherries are sometimes available by the quart or gallon. They deteriorate quickly, so divide among freezer containers and store in freezer until ready to use.)

8 to 10 servings

Almond Cookie Crust
1½ cups unbleached all purpose flour
¼ cup cake flour
¼ cup sugar
¼ cup toasted slivered almonds
 Pinch of salt
½ cup (1 stick) well-chilled unsalted butter, cut into small pieces

1 egg
½ to 1 teaspoon water
1 teaspoon vanilla
½ teaspoon almond extract

Sour Cherry and Marzipan Filling*
2¾ pounds sour cherries, pitted and well drained
¾ cup sugar
¼ cup cornstarch
1½ teaspoons vanilla
 Pinch of salt

¾ cup (6 ounces) canned almond paste
 Powdered sugar

1 egg, well beaten

For crust: Combine flours, sugar, almonds and salt in processor and mix until nuts are finely ground, about 1 minute. Add pieces of butter and blend using several on/off turns until mixture resembles coarse meal.

Beat 1 egg, ½ teaspoon water, vanilla and almond extract in small bowl. Add to nut mixture and blend using on/off turns until dough just begins to gather into ball. If mixture is dry, add remaining ½ teaspoon water; *do not overmix.* Wrap dough in plastic and refrigerate overnight. Let dough stand at room temperature 30 minutes before using.

(To mix crust by hand, grind almonds in blender or mill. Combine with flours, sugar and salt in large bowl. Cut in butter using pastry blender until mixture resembles coarse meal. Add beaten egg, water and extracts, tossing with fork; do not overmix. Wrap dough in plastic and refrigerate overnight. Let dough stand at room temperature about 30 minutes before using.)

Generously butter 9-inch fluted tart pan with removable bottom. Flour work surface and roll ⅓ of dough into 10-inch circle. Place in bottom of tart pan, leaving ½-inch overlap. Refrigerate. Roll out remaining dough and cut into 10-inch round, reserving scraps. Transfer to waxed paper and chill.

For filling: Combine cherries, sugar, cornstarch, vanilla and salt in medium bowl and set aside.

Flatten almond paste into thick round. Generously sprinkle work surface and almond paste with powdered sugar. Roll almond paste out to thickness of less than ⅛ inch; trim to 9-inch circle. (Excess almond paste can be frozen.)

Fill prepared crust with half of cherry mixture. Arrange almond paste circle over cherries. Spread with remaining cherry mixture. Moisten border of overlap with water or some of beaten egg. Cover cherries with remaining 10-inch round of dough. Pinch edges together and fold over onto top crust to free dough from tart pan. Brush top of tart lightly with beaten egg.

Position rack in lower third of oven and preheat to 400°F. Roll out reserved pastry scraps. Using sharp knife, cut 5 large 3 × 1-inch ovals to resemble leaves. Using tip of knife, trace leaf pattern on each oval. Arrange on one side of tart, gently pressing into top crust. Roll out 6 × 1-inch strip and turn in tight spiral to fashion rose. Set in center of leaves. Cut long thin strip of dough to resemble stem and set under rose. Brush decoration with beaten egg.

Using sharp knife, cut several slits around decoration. Set tart on heavy baking sheet and bake until cherries are bubbly, covering crust lightly with foil if it begins to brown too quickly, about 45 minutes to 1 hour. Cool tart on rack about 2 hours. Unmold onto platter.

Tart can be prepared up to 8 hours ahead.

*If sour cherries are unavailable, apricots may be substituted:

Apricot Filling

1½ pounds dried apricots, chopped   ⅔ to 1 cup sugar
   Warm water

Combine apricots in medium bowl with enough warm water to cover and let stand until softened, about 45 minutes. Drain well, reserving 1½ cups liquid. Combine apricots, reserved liquid and ⅔ cup sugar in heavy saucepan. Cover partially, place over medium-high heat and bring to boil. Cook until apricots are soft but not mushy, stirring frequently to prevent sticking, about 10 to 12 minutes. Taste and add more sugar if necesary. Let cool completely. Fill tarts as for cherry and marzipan filling.

Cranberry-Apple Tart with Pecan Streusel

Make the filling at least one day before baking the tart.

10 servings

Crust
2 cups unbleached all purpose flour
   Pinch of salt
6 tablespoons (¾ stick) well-chilled unsalted butter, cut into small pieces
¼ cup well-chilled solid vegetable shortening, cut into small pieces
4 to 5 tablespoons ice water

Cranberry-Apple Filling
1¼ cups unsweetened apple cider or juice
1⅓ cups sugar
4 medium-size tart apples (such as Granny Smith), peeled, cored and cut into ½-inch chunks
12 ounces cranberries

Pecan Streusel
½ cup pecans, finely chopped
½ cup all purpose flour
⅓ cup firmly packed dark brown sugar
6 tablespoons (¾ stick) unsalted butter, melted

Whipped cream

For crust: Combine flour and salt in large bowl. Cut in butter and shortening until mixture resembles coarse meal. Mix in enough water to form ball. Turn dough out onto lightly floured surface. With heel of hand, smear dough a little at a time across surface. Gather into ball, then flatten into disc. Wrap dough with plastic and refrigerate at least 1 hour. (*Can be prepared 3 days ahead.*)

For filling: Heat cider and sugar in heavy large saucepan over low heat, stirring until sugar dissolves. Increase heat and bring to boil. Reduce heat and simmer 2 minutes. Stir in apples and cranberries. Return to boil. Reduce heat and simmer until cranberries burst and apples are tender, stirring frequently, 8 to 10 minutes. Transfer to bowl and cool. Wrap tightly and refrigerate overnight. (*Can be prepared 3 days ahead.*)

Bring filling to room temperature.

Roll dough out on lightly floured surface to ⅛-inch-thick round. Transfer to 10-inch tart pan with removable straight sides. Trim and finish edges. Refrigerate 30 minutes.

Position rack in center of oven and preheat to 400°F. Pierce crust lightly with fork. Line with foil or parchment and fill with dried beans or pie weights. Bake 15 minutes. Remove beans and foil. Continue baking until crust is light brown, about 10 minutes. Cool completely on rack. Reduce temperature to 375°F.

For streusel: Mix first 4 ingredients in large bowl until blended and crumbly.

Place baking sheet on center oven rack and heat 5 minutes. Spoon filling into crust. Sprinkle streusel evenly over filling. Place tart on hot baking sheet and cook until top is brown and filling bubbles, 30 to 35 minutes. Cool completely on rack. Serve with whipped cream.

Green Grape Tart

8 to 10 servings

Crust
- 1 cup sifted all purpose flour
- ½ teaspoon salt
- ⅓ cup well-chilled solid vegetable shortening
- 3 tablespoons ice water

Almond Cream Filling
- 6 tablespoons sugar
- 2 egg yolks

- ¼ cup (½ stick) unsalted butter, room temperature
- ½ cup ground almonds
  Finely grated peel of 1 lemon

- ½ cup apricot preserves
- ¼ cup Grand Marnier
  Green grapes

For crust: Sift flour with salt into large bowl. Cut in shortening until mixture resembles coarse meal. Sprinkle with water and toss with fork until uniformly moistened. Form into ball. Transfer to plastic bag and flatten into disc. Refrigerate for at least 1 hour.

Preheat oven to 400°F. Roll dough on lightly floured surface to thickness of ⅛ inch. Fit into 9-inch tart pan, easing and pressing into place around bottom and sides. With kitchen shears, trim dough ¼ inch beyond pan. Crimp edge, extending ¼ inch above pan to allow for shrinkage during baking.

Line pastry with parchment or waxed paper. Fill with dried beans, rice or pie weights and bake 15 minutes. Remove from oven; discard paper and weights. Reduce oven temperature to 350°F and let crust cool while preparing filling.

For filling: Combine sugar and yolks in medium bowl and beat until pale yellow. Beat in butter. Blend in nuts and lemon peel. Pour into crust and bake until center is golden brown and filling is set, about 10 minutes.

Meanwhile, combine preserves and liqueur in processor or blender and mix thoroughly. Remove tart from oven. Working from outer edge, arrange grapes over top in single layer, covering filling completely. Brush with preserve mixture. Let cool before serving.

The Great Grape-Date Tart

The crust is spread with a rich date paste, then with vanilla pastry cream.

12 servings

Pastry
- 1½ cups all purpose flour
- ½ cup (1 stick) well-chilled unsalted butter, cut into ½-inch pieces
- 2 tablespoons sugar
- 2 egg yolks
  Pinch of salt
- ¼ cup ice water

Vanilla Pastry Cream
- 1½ cups milk
- ½ vanilla bean, split lengthwise
- ½ cup sugar

- 4 extra-large egg yolks, room temperature
- 3 tablespoons all purpose flour

- 2 pounds California dates (preferably Medjool), pitted
- 3 tablespoons (or more) ice water
- 1 teaspoon vanilla
- 20 Thompson seedless grapes
- 20 red flame seedless grapes

- ¼ cup apricot jam, pureed
  Kirsch

For pastry: Combine flour, butter, sugar, yolks and salt in processor and mix, using on/off turns, until consistency of coarse meal. With machine running, pour ice water through feed tube and mix just until dough starts to form ball. Turn dough out onto work surface and form ball; flatten into disc. Wrap in plastic; refrigerate 1 to 2 hours.

Butter 11-inch tart pan with removable bottom. Roll dough out on lightly floured surface to ⅛-inch thickness. Transfer to pan; trim and form decorative edge. Prick bottom with fork. Refrigerate pastry shell 30 minutes.

Preheat oven to 400°F. Line pastry shell with buttered parchment. Fill with dried beans or aluminum pie weights. Bake 10 minutes. Remove beans and paper. Prick crust again and bake until well browned, about 15 more minutes. Let cool.

For pastry cream: Bring milk and vanilla bean to boil in large saucepan. Meanwhile, beat sugar and yolks in large bowl of electric mixer until pale and slowly dissolving ribbon forms when beaters are lifted, 5 to 7 minutes. Mix in flour. Remove vanilla bean from milk. Gradually beat hot milk into egg mixture. Pour custard back into saucepan. Bring to boil over medium heat, stirring constantly until thickened, about 5 minutes. Remove from heat. Press piece of waxed paper onto surface of pastry cream to prevent skin from forming; let cool.

Mix ⅓ of dates, 1 tablespoon ice water and ⅓ teaspoon vanilla in processor to smooth paste, adding more water ⅓ teaspoon at a time as necessary. Repeat twice. Spread date paste onto bottom of pastry shell. Top with pastry cream. Slice grapes lengthwise, then arrange grapes decoratively atop tart.

Melt jam in small saucepan over low heat. Strain into bowl. Thin with small amount of kirsch. Brush glaze over grapes and serve.

Crème Brûlée Tart Jimmy

A layer of uncooked blackberries is sandwiched between pastry and a sour cream custard. The tart is sprinkled with brown sugar, broiled and then chilled, so the guests break through crunchy caramel to the berries and smooth custard.

8 to 10 servings

Pâte Sucrée
- 1 cup all purpose flour
- 2½ tablespoons sugar
- Pinch of salt
- 7 tablespoons well-chilled unsalted butter, cut into ½-inch pieces
- 1 egg yolk

Crème
- 6 egg yolks, room temperature
- 6 tablespoons sugar

- 2 cups whipping cream
- 1 cup sour cream
- 1 teaspoon vanilla
- ¼ cup (½ stick) unsalted butter, cut into pieces, room temperature

- 3 ounces semisweet chocolate, melted
- 2 cups blackberries
- Brown sugar

For pâte: Combine flour, sugar and salt in large bowl. Cut in butter until mixture resembles coarse meal. Add yolk and mix until dough just holds together. Flatten into disc. Wrap in plastic. Refrigerate 1 hour (*or up to 3 days*).

Butter 8- or 9-inch cake pan. Roll dough out on lightly floured surface into circle ⅛ inch thick. Fit into pan; trim and form edges. Prick shell and freeze until firm (*or up to 1 month*).

Preheat oven to 400°F. Line shell with buttered parchment paper and fill with dried beans or pie weights. Bake 15 minutes. Reduce oven temperature to 350°F and bake 10 minutes. Remove paper and weights. Continue baking until brown, about 8 minutes.

For crème: Whisk yolks and sugar in bowl set over pan of gently simmering water (water should not touch bottom of bowl). Add cream, sour cream and vanilla and continue cooking, whisking occasionally, until very thick, 30 to 35 minutes; do not boil or custard will curdle. Remove bowl from over water and whisk in butter. Cool 20 minutes.

To assemble: Preheat broiler. Spread melted chocolate over crust. Cover with berries. Top with custard, smoothing surface with spatula. Sift brown sugar over entire top. Broil until sugar caramelizes, watching carefully to prevent burning. Let cool; refrigerate. Serve tart well chilled.

Lemon Curd and Fresh Blueberry Tart

The blueberries in this tart remain uncooked, fresh and juicy.

8 servings

Lemon Curd
- 10 tablespoons sugar
- 4 egg yolks, room temperature
- 6 tablespoons fresh lemon juice
- ¼ cup (½ stick) unsalted butter, cut into pieces
  Pinch of salt
- 2 teaspoons finely shredded lemon peel (yellow part only)

  Pâte Brisée (see page 2)

Blueberry Topping
- ⅓ cup sugar
- 1 tablespoon arrowroot*
- ½ cup water
- 1½ teaspoons fresh lemon juice
- 3 cups fresh blueberries

For lemon curd: Beat sugar and yolks to blend in heavy nonaluminum saucepan. Add lemon juice, butter and salt. Stir over medium-low heat until mixture thickly coats back of spoon, about 8 minutes; do not boil. Immediately strain into airtight container, pressing with back of spoon to extract as much custard as possible. Mix in lemon peel. Cool. Cover and refrigerate at least 1 hour. (*Can be prepared 1 week ahead.*)

Roll out pâte brisée between sheets of floured plastic wrap or foil to 12-inch round. Without removing plastic wrap, place pastry on baking sheet. Freeze 5 minutes to firm.

Transfer pastry to 10-inch tart pan, removing plastic. Fold pastry over to create double thickness around edge. Cover and refrigerate at least 1 hour.

Freeze pastry 15 minutes.

Preheat oven to 425°F. Line pastry with foil or parchment and fill with pie weights or dried beans. Remove foil and weights. Pierce pastry all over with fork. Bake until pale golden brown, about 5 minutes. Cool on rack.

Spread lemon curd in crust. Set aside.

For topping: Combine sugar and arrowroot in heavy medium saucepan. Mix in water and lemon juice. Stir over medium heat until mixture thickens and turns translucent. Remove from heat. Mix in blueberries, coating well.

Immediately transfer berries to tart, using slotted spoon. Refrigerate at least 30 minutes before serving.

Tart can be prepared 2 hours ahead.

*Cornstarch can be substituted. Cook as above, bringing mixture to full rolling boil.

Blueberry Tart

8 to 10 servings

Pastry
1½ cups all purpose flour
 6 tablespoons (³⁄₄ stick) butter, cut into small pieces
 2 tablespoons solid vegetable shortening
 1 tablespoon sugar
 3 tablespoons ice water

Sauce
 2 cups blueberries
½ cup sugar mixed with
½ teaspoon cornstarch

¼ cup fresh lemon juice
 1 tablespoon red currant jelly
 1 teaspoon finely grated lemon peel

Apricot Glaze
 1 11-ounce jar apricot preserves
¼ cup apricot brandy or orange liqueur

 2 cups blueberries
 Whipping cream

For pastry: Combine flour, butter, shortening and sugar in medium bowl and mix well. Add ice water, stirring with fork until mixture is consistency of coarse meal. Form dough into ball. Knead on floured surface several seconds. Shape into ball and dust with flour. Wrap in waxed paper and refrigerate 1 hour.

Roll dough into 9-inch circle. Press into bottom and sides of 9-inch pie plate or tart pan. Trim excess dough 1 inch beyond rim of pan. Turn excess under to make narrow rolled rim. Flute decoratively or press edge with fork. Prick bottom of pastry and chill for 1 hour.

Position rack in lower third of oven and preheat to 400°F. Line pastry with waxed paper and fill with dried beans or rice. Bake until delicately browned, about 10 to 15 minutes. Discard paper and beans; let tart shell cool.

For sauce: Combine ingredients in medium saucepan and bring to boil over medium heat, stirring frequently. Cook, stirring constantly, until thickened, about 10 minutes. Let cool completely. Transfer to bowl and chill.

For glaze: Combine preserves and brandy in processor or blender and puree. Brush thin layer over tart shell. (Store remaining glaze in refrigerator.)

Spread remaining 2 cups blueberries in shell. Carefully pour sauce over top. Chill until set. Serve with cream.

Philly Blue-Apple Pie

8 servings

Crust
 1 cup all purpose flour
 1 teaspoon sugar
 1 teaspoon salt
¼ cup solid vegetable shortening, cut into pieces
¼ cup (½ stick) well-chilled unsalted butter, cut into pieces
 3 to 4 tablespoons ice water

Filling
 2 cups sliced, peeled tart apple (about 2 large apples)

 2 cups fresh blueberries, stemmed
 1 cup sugar
 2 tablespoons all purpose flour
 2 teaspoons butter, cut into pieces
½ teaspoon cinnamon
¼ teaspoon freshly grated nutmeg
 2 to 3 tablespoons fresh lemon juice (1 small lemon)

Topping
 2 tablespoons all purpose flour
 2 tablespoons (¼ stick) butter
 1 tablespoon sugar

For crust: Preheat oven to 450°F. Combine flour, sugar and salt in medium bowl. Cut in shortening and butter until mixture resembles coarse meal. Add ice water and mix to form dough. Transfer to lightly floured surface. Roll dough out to thickness of ⅛ inch. Fit dough into 9-inch metal pie pan, fluting edges. Set aside.

For filling: Combine apple, blueberries, sugar, flour, butter, cinnamon and nutmeg in large bowl. Add lemon juice and toss well. Spoon mixture into prepared pie shell.

For topping: Mix flour, butter and sugar in small bowl. Sprinkle over fruit mixture. Bake pie 15 minutes. Reduce oven temperature to 350°F and continue baking for 30 more minutes. Serve pie warm.

Blueberry Walnut Pie

8 to 10 servings

2½ cups graham cracker crumbs
½ cup finely chopped walnuts
6 tablespoons (¾ stick) butter, melted
3 tablespoons honey
½ teaspoon cinnamon

6 egg yolks
1 cup blueberry juice (drained from canned blueberries)
1 cup whipping cream
½ cup sugar
½ teaspoon cinnamon

2 tablespoons fresh lemon juice
1 teaspoon vanilla

¼ cup blueberry juice (drained from canned blueberries)
1 envelope unflavored gelatin

1 cup whipping cream
2 cups canned blueberries
1 cup walnuts, chopped and toasted
Whipped cream

For crust: Preheat oven to 350°F. Combine graham cracker crumbs, ½ cup finely chopped walnuts, butter, honey and cinnamon in large bowl and mix well. Press into 10-inch deep-dish pie pan. Bake 10 minutes. Let cool while preparing filling.

Combine egg yolks, 1 cup blueberry juice, 1 cup whipping cream, sugar and cinnamon in 2-quart saucepan. Cook over medium heat, whisking constantly, until mixture coats back of spoon or registers 180°F, about 8 to 10 minutes; do not boil. Immediately pour into large bowl of electric mixer. Add lemon juice and vanilla and beat on low speed until egg yolk mixture begins to cool, approximately 3 to 5 minutes.

Meanwhile, combine ¼ cup blueberry juice and gelatin in small saucepan and stir over low heat until gelatin is dissolved, about 2 minutes. Add small amount of cooling yolk mixture and blend well. Slowly add gelatin mixture to egg yolk mixture and blend well. Refrigerate, stirring frequently, until mousse just begins to thicken and set.

Whip 1 cup cream in large bowl of electric mixer until stiff peaks form. Fold cream and blueberries into mousse. Spoon into prepared crust. Cover entire top of pie with chopped toasted walnuts. Refrigerate until completely set, about 2 to 3 hours. Top each serving with whipped cream.

Cookie Crust Tart with Boysenberry Puree

8 servings

Cookie Crust
½ cup sliced blanched almonds
5 tablespoons sugar
1¼ cups (2½ sticks) unsalted butter
2½ tablespoons almond paste
1 jumbo egg yolk
1½ cups plus 2 tablespoons all purpose flour

Boysenberry Puree
4 cups boysenberries
¾ cup sugar, or more to taste
1 teaspoon fresh lemon juice

Powdered sugar

For crust: Grind almonds with half of sugar in processor. Beat ground almonds, remaining sugar, butter, almond paste and egg yolk in large bowl of electric mixer until light and fluffy. Blend in flour just until mixture forms ball; do not overmix. Flatten into disc. Wrap dough in plastic or waxed paper and refrigerate while making puree.

For puree: Puree berries in processor or blender. Transfer to heavy medium saucepan. Add sugar and lemon juice and stir over medium heat until thick, about 12 minutes. Strain puree through very fine sieve.

To assemble: Place 9-inch flan ring or tart pan with removable bottom on baking sheet. Spoon dough into pastry bag fitted with No. 6 tip and pipe (if too sticky to pipe, add a bit more flour) in concentric circle to cover bottom of pan, then pipe around side. Refrigerate for 30 minutes.

Preheat oven to 375°F. Spoon puree into crust. Pipe lattice design over top with remaining dough. Bake until crisp and golden, about 45 minutes. Before serving, dust with powdered sugar.

Marzipan Tart

Adorned with fresh boysenberries, this tart is best served on the day it is prepared.

8 to 10 servings

Pâte Sucrée
1½ cups all purpose flour
¼ cup sugar
    Pinch of salt
10 tablespoons (1¼ sticks) chilled unsalted butter, cut into ½-inch pieces
1 egg

Marzipan Filling
½ cup (1 stick) unsalted butter, room temperature

8 ounces almond paste, room temperature
2 eggs, room temperature
3 tablespoons Cognac
2 teaspoons all purpose flour

5 cups fresh boysenberries
1 12-ounce jar boysenberry jam, melted, strained and heated with dash of Cognac

For pâte: Combine flour, sugar and salt in large bowl. Cut in butter until mixture resembles coarse meal. Add egg and mix until dough just holds together. Flatten into disc. Wrap tightly in plastic and chill at least 1 hour (*or up to 3 days*).

Butter 11-inch tart pan. Roll dough out on lightly floured surface into 13-inch circle ⅛ inch thick. Fit into pan; trim and form edges. Prick with fork. Freeze until firm (*or up to 1 month*).

Preheat oven to 425°F. Line pastry shell with buttered parchment paper, then fill with dried beans or pie weights. Bake 5 minutes. Reduce oven temperature to 350°F and continue baking 15 minutes. Remove paper and weights. Bake until pastry browns, about 10 minutes. Cool while preparing filling. Retain oven at 350°F.

For filling: Cream butter and almond paste in medium bowl. Beat in eggs one at a time. Blend in Cognac and flour. Pour into crust. Bake until filling is dry and light brown, about 30 minutes. Cool completely. (*Can be prepared early on day of serving to this point and stored at room temperature.*)

To serve, arrange berries atop filling. Brush with melted jam, thinning glaze with additional Cognac if necessary.

Fruit Tarte Renversée

8 servings

Sweet Pastry
1²/₃ cups pastry flour
2 tablespoons sugar
1 teaspoon grated lemon peel
¹/₈ teaspoon salt
9 tablespoons well-chilled unsalted butter
1 egg yolk
1 to 3 tablespoons ice water
1 tablespoon fresh lemon juice

Apple and Pear Filling
2 pounds Pippin or Granny Smith apples, peeled, cored and cut into ³/₈-inch-thick slices
2 tablespoons fresh lemon juice

1¹/₄ pounds ripe but firm Anjou pears, peeled, cored and cut into ³/₈- to ¹/₂-inch-thick slices
4 tablespoons (¹/₂ stick) butter
2 tablespoons Calvados or brandy
¹/₄ cup sugar
1 teaspoon grated lemon peel
¹/₂ teaspoon cinnamon
¹/₂ teaspoon freshly grated nutmeg

Caramel
²/₃ cup sugar
¹/₄ cup water
¹/₃ cup toasted husked hazelnuts, coarsely chopped

For pastry: Mix flour, sugar, lemon peel and salt in medium bowl. Cut in butter until coarse meal forms. Make well in center of dry ingredients. Add yolk, 1 tablespoon of water and lemon juice to well and blend with fork. Mix into dry ingredients, adding remaining water if necessary to bind dough. Using heel of hand, smear dough a little at a time across lightly floured surface. Gather into ball; flatten into disc. Wrap dough in waxed paper and refrigerate at least 1 hour.

For filling: Mix apples with 1 tablespoon lemon juice in medium bowl. Mix pears with remaining 1 tablespoon lemon juice in another medium bowl. Melt 2 tablespoons butter in heavy large skillet over medium heat. Add apples and cook until beginning to soften, stirring frequently, about 5 minutes. Transfer to colander set over bowl. Repeat with remaining 2 tablespoons butter and pears. Return drained apple and pear juices to skillet. Add Calvados and bring to boil, scraping up any browned bits. Mix in sugar, lemon peel, cinnamon and nutmeg. Boil until thick and syrupy, stirring constantly, about 3 minutes. Set Calvados syrup aside.

For caramel: Cook sugar and water in heavy small saucepan over low heat, swirling pan occasionally, until sugar dissolves. Increase heat to medium and boil until dark caramel color. Immediately pour caramel into 10-inch pie pan, tilting pan to coat bottom.

Sprinkle hazelnuts evenly over caramel. Let stand until caramel is firm.

Preheat oven to 375°F. Arrange some of apples around outer edge of pan, overlapping slightly. Overlap pears in ring next to apples. Repeat with remaining apples. Fill in spaces with any remaining fruit. Pour syrup over.

Roll dough out on lightly floured surface to 12-inch round. Place over fruit. Trim and crimp edges. Cut 5 small slits in dough. Bake until crust is well browned and fruit is caramel colored, covering crust with foil if browning too quickly, about 1 hour. Cool in pan 5 minutes. Invert tart onto platter. Serve warm or at room temperature.

Fresh Kiwi Tart

Almost any fresh fruit—strawberries, sliced oranges, grapes—can be substituted for the kiwis in this easy but elegant dessert.

6 servings

1 cup all purpose flour
2 tablespoons powdered sugar
½ cup (1 stick) well-chilled butter
2 to 3 tablespoons ice water

1 cup apple jelly
2 tablespoons Grand Marnier or fresh orange juice
6 kiwis, peeled and sliced

Sift flour and sugar into large bowl. Cut in butter using pastry blender or two knives until mixture resembles coarse meal. Mix in enough water to bind ingredients. Wrap dough in plastic and refrigerate 30 minutes.

Preheat oven to 425°F. Roll dough out on lightly floured surface to thickness of ⅛ inch. Transfer to 9-inch tart pan with removable bottom, pressing into sides and trimming excess. Pierce bottom of dough with fork. Bake until golden brown, 15 to 18 minutes. Cool crust to room temperature.

Simmer jelly and Grand Marnier in heavy small saucepan until jelly melts, stirring constantly. Brush about ½ cup over bottom of crust. Arrange kiwi slices in crust, overlapping slightly. Spoon remaining jelly mixture evenly over kiwi. Refrigerate tart until jelly mixture is set.

Raspberry Tart Plaza-Athénée

6 to 8 servings

Pastry
5 tablespoons unsalted butter, room temperature
⅔ cup powdered sugar
1 egg yolk, room temperature
1 tablespoon milk
2 teaspoons grated lemon peel
½ teaspoon vanilla
Pinch of salt
1 cup all purpose flour

Filling
½ cup ground toasted blanched almonds
¼ cup ground toasted husked hazelnuts

¼ cup (½ stick) unsalted butter, room temperature
¼ cup sugar
1 tablespoon all purpose flour
1 egg
1 egg yolk
1 teaspoon vanilla
¼ teaspoon almond extract
2 tablespoons raspberry liqueur or brandy or Cognac

2 cups fresh raspberries
Powdered sugar

For pastry: Cream butter and sugar. Mix in yolk, milk, peel, vanilla and salt. Add flour and stir until just combined; do not overmix. Gather dough into ball. Wrap in plastic. Chill 1 hour.

Roll dough out on lightly floured surface to thickness of ⅛ inch. Set in 9-inch fluted tart pan with removable bottom; trim edges. Chill 30 minutes.

Preheat oven to 400°F. Place tart pan on baking sheet. Line shell with parchment or foil. Fill with dried beans or pie weights. Bake until sides are set, about 10 minutes. Remove beans and foil. Bake until brown, about 10 minutes. Reduce temperature to 375°F.

Meanwhile, prepare filling: Mix almonds, hazelnuts, butter, sugar, flour, egg, yolk, vanilla and almond extract. Spread in shell. Bake 5 minutes. Brush with liqueur. Cool completely on rack.

Before serving, arrange raspberries atop filling. Dust with powdered sugar.

Papa Haydn's Raspberry Tart

6 to 8 servings

Walnut Pastry
½ cup (1 stick) butter, room temperature
2½ tablespoons sugar
½ cup finely chopped walnuts
1 egg, beaten to blend
1 teaspoon almond extract
1⅓ cups all purpose flour

Vanilla Custard
2 egg yolks, room temperature
2½ tablespoons sugar

2 tablespoons cornstarch
½ teaspoon vanilla
⅔ cup milk
6 tablespoons (¾ stick) butter, room temperature

4 cups fresh raspberries

1 cup red currant jelly
1 cup whipping cream, whipped

For pastry: Butter 10- or 11-inch tart pan with removable bottom. Cream ½ cup butter and sugar in large bowl. Mix in walnuts. Blend in egg and almond extract. Stir in flour until fully incorporated. Press dough into pan. Chill 30 minutes.

Preheat oven to 350°F. Bake shell until golden brown, 15 to 20 minutes. Cool pie crust to room temperature.

For custard: Beat yolks, sugar, cornstarch and vanilla in medium bowl until pale and thick. Heat milk in heavy medium saucepan. Beat milk into yolk mixture until smooth. Return mixture to saucepan and whisk over medium heat until very thick, about 5 minutes. Return mixture to bowl and beat until cool. Beat in butter 1 tablespoon at a time. Refrigerate until chilled.

To assemble: Spread custard evenly over bottom of crust. Starting from outside edge, arrange berries in concentric circles over custard, placing berries as close together as possible. Refrigerate 30 minutes.

Melt red currant jelly in heavy small saucepan over low heat, stirring occasionally. Brush gently over berries, covering completely. Refrigerate at least 2 hours. Serve tart with whipped cream.

Lemon Raspberry Tart

8 to 10 servings

Pastry
2 cups all purpose flour
2 tablespoons sugar
1 teaspoon grated lemon peel
Pinch of salt
½ cup (1 stick) well-chilled unsalted butter, cut into ½-inch pieces
3 tablespoons chilled solid vegetable shortening
1 tablespoon Cognac
2 to 4 tablespoons ice water

Lemon Filling
1½ cups sugar

½ cup (1 stick) unsalted butter, melted and cooled
7 tablespoons fresh lemon juice
3 extra-large eggs, room temperature, beaten to blend
2 egg yolks, room temperature, beaten to blend
1 to 2 tablespoons minced lemon peel

4 cups fresh raspberries

For pastry: Combine flour, sugar, peel and salt in large bowl. Cut in butter and shortening until mixture resembles coarse meal. Add Cognac, then gradually blend in water until mixture can be gathered into ball. Flatten dough into disc. Wrap in plastic and refrigerate 1 hour (*or up to 3 days*).

Butter 10- to 11-inch quiche pan. Roll dough out on lightly floured surface into 12- to 13-inch circle ⅛ inch thick. Fit into pan; form edges. Freeze until firm (*or up to 1 month*).

Preheat oven to 450°F. Prick pastry shell with fork. Line with buttered parchment paper, then fill with dried beans or pie weights. Bake 5 minutes. Reduce oven temperature to 350°F and bake 10 minutes. Remove paper and weights. Continue baking until well browned, about 20 minutes.

For filling: Combine all ingredients in heavy medium saucepan and stir constantly over low heat until thick, 15 to 20 minutes; do not boil. Let cool. (*Can be prepared 2 days ahead. Place plastic wrap directly on surface of filling after cooling. Refrigerate until ready to use.*)

Spoon filling into crust. Arrange raspberries decoratively over top and serve.

Raspberry-filled Meringue Tarts

2 servings

Meringues
- 1 **egg white, room temperature**
- 1/4 **teaspoon cream of tartar**
- **Pinch of salt**
- 5 **tablespoons sugar**
- 1/4 **teaspoon almond extract**
- 1 **tablespoon blanched almonds, minced**

Raspberry Filling
- 1 **cup raspberries**
- 1/4 **cup sugar**
- 2 **tablespoons red currant jelly**
- 1 **tablespoon kirsch**
- 1 1/2 **teaspoons Grand Marnier**

For meringues: Preheat oven to 225°F. Line baking sheet with parchment paper. Beat egg white in medium bowl until foamy. Add cream of tartar and salt and continue beating until soft peaks form. Add sugar 1 tablespoon at a time, beating until sugar is dissolved. Blend in extract. Gently fold in nuts.

Using rubber spatula, spread meringue mixture into 2 circles on parchment paper, each circle about 3 inches in diameter and 1 1/2 to 2 inches high, spacing well apart. Built up outer edges to form hollow center in each meringue. Bake 1 hour. Turn off heat and let meringues cool in oven with door ajar. Carefully remove meringues from parchment paper using spatula.

For filling: Combine 1/2 cup raspberries and 1/4 cup sugar in processor or blender and puree until smooth, about 3 minutes, stopping as necessary to scrape down sides of container. Press puree through fine strainer set over medium bowl to remove seeds.

Combine jelly and liqueurs in small saucepan. Place over low heat and warm until jelly is liquefied. Blend into raspberry puree. Gently stir in remaining whole berries. Chill thoroughly.

To serve, transfer meringues to individual dessert plates. Spoon raspberry mixture evenly into centers, allowing some of puree to run down sides.

Glazed Strawberry Pie

8 servings

- 1 **cup fresh strawberries**
- **Water**
- 1/2 to 3/4 **cup sugar**
- **Pinch of salt**
- 1 **teaspoon cornstarch dissolved in**
- 1 **tablespoon water**
- 1 **baked 9-inch pie crust**
- 2 **cups (or more) strawberries, hulled**
- **Softly whipped cream**

Crush 1 cup strawberries; add enough water to equal 1 cup. Strain. Combine with sugar and salt in small saucepan and simmer, stirring constantly, until sugar is dissolved. Slowly stir in dissolved cornstarch and cook until clear and slightly thickened. Let cool slightly. Brush bottom of pie shell with some of glaze. Arrange remaining berries pointed ends up in shell. Pour remaining glaze over top. Chill 2 to 3 hours or overnight. Top with softly whipped cream or pass separately.

Strawberry-glazed Sherry Pie

8 to 10 servings

3 eggs
2 cups half and half
½ cup dry Sherry
½ cup sugar
1 baked 9-inch pie crust
1 egg white, beaten to blend

Strawberry Glaze
½ cup red currant jelly
2 teaspoons hot water

1 pint whole fresh strawberries, hulled

Position rack in lower third of oven and preheat to 325°F. Lightly beat eggs in mixing bowl just enough to incorporate whites and yolks. Add half and half, Sherry and sugar and stir until sugar is dissolved. Brush pastry with egg white to waterproof crust. Let dry 2 minutes. Pour in filling. Bake until custard is set, 1 to 1½ hours. Let cool, then chill.

For glaze: Combine jelly and water in small saucepan and stir over low heat until jelly is melted and mixture is smooth.

Arrange strawberries, pointed side up, in concentric circles over top of pie. Using pastry brush, lightly coat each berry with glaze. Chill before serving.

Fresh Strawberry Custard Tart

8 to 10 servings

Pastry
11 tablespoons well-chilled unsalted butter, cut into 12 pieces
½ cup powdered sugar
1 egg
½ egg yolk
1 tablespoon water
2 teaspoons vanilla
Pinch of salt
1½ cups plus 2 tablespoons unbleached all purpose flour

Vanilla Custard
4 eggs
1 cup sugar
1 teaspoon vanilla or to taste
Pinch of salt
1¼ cups whipping cream

Strawberry Topping
½ cup red currant jelly
1 pint fresh strawberries, hulled and sliced

For pastry: Combine all ingredients except flour in processor and mix using 6 on/off turns, then process 5 seconds (small pieces of butter will remain). Add flour and process just until dough begins to mass together; *do not let dough form ball.* Place dough in plastic bag. Press into ball, then flatten into disc. Refrigerate at least 2 hours or overnight.

Butter 11-inch tart pan with removable bottom. Roll pastry out on lightly floured surface into circle about ⅛ inch thick. Press onto bottom and sides of prepared pan. Trim dough 1 inch beyond edge of pan. Fold inch under to form double thickness on sides. Press firmly into place with pastry extending ¼ inch above edge of pan. Crimp edge decoratively. Prick bottom and sides of crust with fork. Refrigerate until firm, about 30 minutes.

Position rack in center of oven and preheat to 400°F. Line pastry with parchment and fill with dried beans, rice or pie weights. Bake until just set, about 12 minutes. Remove paper and beans, prick crust again and continue baking until bottom of crust is lightly browned, about 10 to 15 minutes (cover edges with foil if necessary).

Meanwhile, prepare custard: Combine eggs, sugar, vanilla and salt in processor and blend 1 minute, stopping to scrape down sides of bowl. With machine running, pour cream through feed tube and mix 5 seconds.

Reduce oven temperature to 325°F. Pour custard into crust. Bake until custard is medium brown and moves only slightly when pan is shaken, about 22 to 24 minutes. Cool crust completely on wire rack.

For topping: Melt currant jelly in small saucepan over low heat. Using soft pastry brush, carefully spread thin layer of melted jelly over surface of cooled custard. Arrange strawberry slices in concentric circles over top, overlapping slightly. Brush strawberries and edge of crust with remaining jelly.

Crust and custard can be baked one day ahead and refrigerated. Bring to room temperature, then add strawberry topping up to several hours before serving.

Strawberry Tart

8 servings

1 pound Whole Wheat Puff Pastry (see next recipe)

1 egg, beaten

2 cups Vanilla Pastry Cream* *or* ³/₄ cup red currant jelly

4 cups whole fresh strawberries, hulled
1 cup red currant jelly
1 tablespoon fresh lemon juice

Turn pastry out onto lightly floured surface and roll to thickness of ³/₁₆ inch. Cut out 12 × 6-inch rectangle; transfer to dampened baking sheet. From remaining pastry, cut two 12 × ¹/₂-inch strips and two 5 x ¹/₂-inch strips. Lightly moisten 1 inch of outer edges of rectangle. Set dough strips atop corresponding edges to form double thickness, moistening with water so strips adhere. Freeze.

Preheat oven to 375°F. Thoroughly prick center of tart (not raised edges) with fork. Brush top of edges with beaten egg. Bake until pastry has risen and is slightly browned, about 30 to 40 minutes. (Check tart after 5 minutes of baking; if bottom is puffed, remove from oven and prick again with fork until dough deflates.) When tart is done, remove from oven and let cool on rack for 20 minutes. Pull out any excess pastry in center so inside is flat.

Transfer tart shell to serving platter. Spread bottom with vanilla pastry cream or ³/₄ cup currant jelly. Arrange strawberries stem end down over filling. Combine 1 cup currant jelly with lemon juice in small saucepan and warm over low heat until dissolved and smooth. Let cool slightly. Carefully coat strawberries with glaze. Refrigerate.

*Vanilla Pastry Cream

Makes about 2 cups

1 egg
1 egg yolk
3 tablespoons unbleached all purpose flour
2 tablespoons light honey
1 tablespoon unflavored gelatin

³/₄ cup milk
¹/₄ vanilla bean, split and scraped, or 1 teaspoon vanilla

2 egg whites
1 cup whipping cream, whipped

Combine egg, egg yolk, flour and honey in medium bowl of electric mixer and beat well. Blend in gelatin. Combine milk and vanilla in small saucepan over medium heat and bring to boil. Slowly stir hot milk into egg mixture.

Return mixture to saucepan. Place over low heat and bring to boil, stirring constantly. Set saucepan in bowl of ice and whisk custard until thickened and cooled. Beat egg whites in small bowl until soft peaks form; fold into custard. Add whipped cream 1 tablespoon at a time, whisking vigorously after each addition, until mixture is creamy.

Pastry cream can be prepared 2 to 3 days ahead and refrigerated.

Whole Wheat Puff Pastry

Hard wheat flour is used because it is high in gluten, which helps make the dough elastic. We suggest that you use the food processor to give the mixture a powerful beating; this activates the gluten. The dough holds together without breaking, even in very thin layers.

Makes 1 pound

2 cups stoneground whole wheat bread flour
½ teaspoon sea salt
⅓ cup plus 2 tablespoons ice water or well-chilled nonfat milk
2 teaspoons fresh lemon juice

1¼ cups (2½ sticks) well-chilled unsalted butter, cut into ½-inch cubes

Combine 1¾ cups flour and salt in processor and mix using 1 to 2 on/off turns. With machine running, add water or milk and lemon juice and mix until dough forms ball, about 2 to 3 minutes. Turn dough out onto *unfloured* surface and shape into smooth ball. Make deep crosscut on top of ball using sharp knife. Cover with plastic wrap and chill in freezer until firm, about 30 minutes.

Meanwhile, combine butter and remaining flour in large bowl and mix until smooth. Turn out onto work surface. Form into 4-inch square using spatula. Cover butter with plastic wrap and chill in freezer until firm, about 20 minutes.

When dough and butter are chilled to equal firmness, but not frozen, transfer dough to lightly floured surface and roll into 12-inch square. Set butter mixture in center of dough and fold sides over butter evenly, making sure ends meet in center. Pinch ends of dough together so there are no holes. Using rolling pin, make series of slight depressions in crisscross pattern over dough until square is flattened to 8 inches. Roll dough into rectangle. Fold top third toward center; fold remaining third over top, as for business letter. *This is a single turn.* Cover with plastic and chill in freezer until firm but not frozen, about 20 minutes.

Turn dough out onto lightly floured surface with open end toward you. Roll into large rectangle about ⅜ inch thick. Fold short ends so they meet at center of dough without overlapping. Fold in half at center. *This is a double turn.* Cover with plastic and chill in freezer until firm but not frozen, about 20 minutes.

Repeat single turn, chilling in freezer until firm but not frozen, about 20 minutes. Repeat double turn 3 more times, chilling in freezer after each. Cover with plastic and refrigerate.

Whole wheat puff pastry can be frozen but is best prepared and baked the same day.

Strawberry Tart with Beurre Noisette

A crisp pâte sucrée *with a rich and buttery filling.*

6 to 8 servings

Pâte Sucrée
1½ cups all purpose flour
¼ cup sugar
   Pinch of salt
10 tablespoons (1¼ sticks) well-chilled unsalted butter, cut into ½-inch pieces
2 egg yolks

Beurre Noisette
2 eggs, room temperature
¾ cup plus 2 teaspoons sugar

¼ cup all purpose flour
¼ cup (½ stick) butter, warmed until medium brown, then cooled
   Dash of vanilla

3 cups thinly sliced strawberries
½ cup strawberry preserves, melted and strained

For pâte: Combine flour, sugar and salt in large bowl. Cut in butter until mixture resembles coarse meal. Add yolks and mix until dough just holds together. Flatten into disc. Wrap tightly in plastic and refrigerate for at least 1 hour (*or for up to 3 days*).

Butter 4½ × 14-inch rectangular flan mold. Roll dough out on lightly floured surface into 8 × 16-inch rectangle ⅛ inch thick. Fit dough into pan, pressing gently; trim and form edges. Freeze until firm (*or up to 1 month*).

For beurre noisette: Preheat oven to 450°F. Whisk eggs, sugar and flour in medium bowl to blend. Add butter and vanilla. Pour into crust. Bake 5 minutes. Reduce oven temperature to 325°F. Bake until firm, 40 to 50 minutes. Cool. (*Can be prepared early on day it will be served and stored at room temperature until ready to use.*)

To assemble: Arrange strawberry slices in overlapping rows atop tart. Brush with preserves. Serve within 2 hours.

Strawberry-Raspberry Chocolate Tart

The crust for this impressive tart can be prepared the day before serving. The remaining raspberry mixture can be used with other fruit tarts, or served warm over scoops of ice cream.

6 to 8 servings

Chocolate Crust
  6 ounces semisweet chocolate
  ¼ cup (½ stick) unsalted butter
  1 cup graham cracker crumbs
  2 tablespoons sugar

Berry Filling
  1 10-ounce package frozen raspberries in syrup, thawed

  2½ tablespoons fresh lemon juice
  2 tablespoons cornstarch
  6 tablespoons sugar
  1 quart fresh strawberries, halved

  1 cup well-chilled whipping cream
  1 teaspoon vanilla

For crust: Preheat oven to 400°F. Melt chocolate and butter in top of double boiler over barely simmering water. Stir until smooth. Combine graham cracker crumbs and sugar in large bowl. Stir in chocolate mixture using 2 forks. Pat mixture evenly over sides and bottom of 9-inch tart pan with removable bottom. Freeze 5 minutes. Bake crust until firm, about 8 minutes. Cool completely. (*Can be prepared 1 day ahead to this point.*)

For filling: Puree raspberries in processor or blender. Strain through fine sieve into heavy small saucepan. Mix lemon juice and cornstarch and whisk into puree. Add sugar. Stir over medium heat until translucent and very thick. Cool until just warm. Add strawberries and stir until well coated. Using slotted spoon, transfer berries to crust and arrange them cut side down with points facing outer edges of crust.

Whip cream and vanilla to form peaks. Spoon into pastry bag fitted with star tip. Pipe rosettes of cream around edge of tart. (*Can be prepared 2 hours ahead and chilled. Let stand at room temperature 15 minutes before serving.*)

Cherimoya, Strawberry and Kiwi Tart with Macadamia Nuts

Light and fanciful, with a crisp nut crust. Serve the same day it is baked.

6 to 8 servings

  1 cup unsalted macadamia nuts, lightly toasted
  ¾ cup sugar
  ½ cup lightly toasted sliced almonds
  ¼ cup lightly toasted shredded unsweetened coconut
  6 egg whites, room temperature
  ½ teaspoon cream of tartar

  1 cherimoya,* peeled, seeded and quartered, or ¼ pineapple, peeled and cut into 1-inch cubes

  6 passion fruits,** peeled
  2 tablespoons sugar

  4 kiwis, peeled and sliced
  12 strawberries, each cut 3 times to form fans, or 2 persimmons, peeled and cut into rounds

To create pattern for torten decorations, cut out telephone receiver-shaped hole in piece of cardboard; stencil should be 9½ inches long, 1¾ inches wide in center and 2½ inches wide at rounded ends.

Preheat oven to 300°F. Generously butter 3 baking sheets and dust with flour. Draw 10-inch circle in center of 1 sheet, using tart pan as guide. Refrigerate sheets until well chilled. Chop macadamia nuts with ¾ cup sugar in processor. Add almonds and grind mixture finely. Add coconut and process to combine. Beat whites and cream of tartar until stiff but not dry. Fold in nuts. Cover circle on prepared sheet with ¼-inch-thick layer of batter. Bake until light brown, about 15 minutes. Trim circle. Transfer tart base to rack and cool.

Place stencil for decorations at one end of prepared sheet. Spread ¹⁄₁₆-inch-thick layer of batter within stencil; remove stencil and repeat, forming 3 decorations on sheets. Bake 1 sheet until decorations are light brown, about 12 minutes. Using spatula or sharp knife, remove 1 decoration from sheet. Hold upright on surface, with 2 rounded ends down. Fold crosswise around clean metal nail to form 45° angle at center. Bend rounded ends to right to form 45° angle with work surface. Hold until firm, about 2 minutes. Place on rack. Fold remaining 2 decorations, returning to oven briefly to soften if necessary. Repeat baking and forming with remaining sheet of decorations. Cool completely.

Cut each cherimoya quarter crosswise into 3 pieces. Slice almost all the way through, forming fans. Puree passion fruits in processor. Strain into heavy small saucepan. Add sugar.

Preheat oven to 250°F. Place round base on ovenproof platter. Arrange 5 or 6 decorations atop base with folded ends together in center. Heat in oven 5 minutes. Bring passion fruit puree to simmer, stirring constantly. Pour puree into small serving bowl.

Arrange fruit decoratively atop base. Serve immediately. Spoon warm passion fruit puree atop each portion.

*A green subtropical fruit with a custardlike texture and mild taste. Available at specialty produce markets.

**½ cup pomegranate juice can be substituted. Boil with 2 tablespoons sugar in heavy small saucepan until syrupy.

Rhubarb and Strawberry Tart

Phyllo pastry makes a light, crisp crust for this delectable tart.

8 to 10 servings

¾ cup (1½ sticks) unsalted butter, melted and cooled
1 pound phyllo pastry sheets
  Sugar
1 egg white, beaten to blend

2 tablespoons dry breadcrumbs
2 cups ½-inch pieces fresh or unsweetened frozen rhubarb, thawed

2 cups strawberries, sliced
1 cup sugar
¼ cup quick-cooking tapioca
1 teaspoon fresh lemon juice
2 tablespoons (¼ stick) well-chilled unsalted butter

Preheat oven to 425°F. Generously butter 9 × 2-inch fluted tart pan with removable bottom. Stack 12 pastry sheets on work surface (cover remainder with dry towel and top with damp towel). Fold left half of pastry stack over right half, forming book. Unfold top sheet. Brush very lightly with melted butter and sprinkle lightly with sugar. Repeat until last sheet on left is opened. *Do not butter.* Fold right side of stack over left side. Open top sheet. Butter and sprinkle with sugar. Repeat until pastry sheets are opened flat. Fit stack of pastry into prepared pan, draping excess pastry over rim. Run rolling pin firmly over pan to cut phyllo. Place pan on baking sheet. Line phyllo with foil and fill with dried beans. Brush phyllo with egg white. Bake until light brown, 3 to 5 minutes. Cool completely

Sprinkle crust with breadcrumbs. Combine rhubarb, strawberries, sugar, tapioca and lemon juice. Spoon into crust. Dot with 2 tablespoons butter.

Butter and sugar 1 remaining phyllo sheet. Cut in half lengthwise. Fold each piece in half lengthwise; butter and sprinkle with sugar. Fold in half lengthwise 2 more times without buttering or sugaring, forming ½- to ¾-inch rolls. Place rolls atop filling around edges of pan. Repeat with remaining pastry sheets, overlapping ends by 1 inch and spiraling in toward center of tart. For center, hold 1 pastry roll between thumb and index finger. Wrap phyllo around fingers, tucking end under. Place in center of tart.

Brush tart with some of remaining melted butter and sprinkle with sugar. Place on baking sheet. Bake until rhubarb is tender and crust is golden brown, 35 to 40 minutes, covering loosely with foil if top browns too quickly. Cool completely on rack. Loosen tart from pan with knife; remove rim. Serve tart at room temperature.

Rhubarb Tarts in Walnut Pastry

2 servings

Pastry
½ cup all purpose flour
½ cup ground walnuts (1 ounce)
2 tablespoons sugar
¼ cup (½ stick) well-chilled unsalted butter, cut into small pieces
1 tablespoon (about) ice water

Filling
⅓ cup water
¼ cup (or more) sugar

1 cup chopped fresh rhubarb*

2 tablespoons water
¾ teaspoon arrowroot

2 to 3 tablespoons red currant jelly
Crème fraîche or sour cream

For pastry: Combine flour, walnuts and sugar in medium bowl. Cut in butter until mixture resembles coarse meal. Blend in water just until dough holds together. Wrap dough in plastic and refrigerate thoroughly.

Preheat oven to 350°F. Roll dough out on lightly floured surface to thickness of ⅛ inch. Cut out two 4½-inch circles. Fit into two 3½-inch round tart pans. Trim edges of dough even with edge of pan. Prick bottom with fork. Bake until crisp and lightly browned, about 25 minutes. Let cool.

For filling: Combine ⅓ cup water and ¼ cup sugar in medium saucepan over low heat. Add rhubarb, cover and bring to simmer, stirring gently once or twice. Cook just until rhubarb is tender, about 3 to 5 minutes. Drain, reserving liquid. Taste and adjust sweetness of rhubarb, adding more sugar if desired. Return liquid to pan.

Mix 2 tablespoons water with arrowroot. Blend into rhubarb cooking liquid, place over low heat and stir gently until thickened and clear, about 5 minutes. Add rhubarb. Let cool.

Spoon filling into tart shells. Melt jelly over very low heat. Spoon or brush evenly over filling. Refrigerate tarts until ready to serve. Top each with dollop of crème fraîche or sour cream.

*A 10-ounce package of thawed frozen rhubarb can be substituted. Drain well, reserving juice; substitute juice for water in filling. Measure 1 cup rhubarb, reserving remainder for another use.

Strawberry Rhubarb Pie

Pastry flowers and a lattice crust decorate this charming spring dessert.

6 to 8 servings

Crust
2½ cups all purpose flour
1 teaspoon salt
1 cup shortening
6 tablespoons ice water

Filling
4 cups fresh strawberries, sliced
1½ cups fresh rhubarb, cut into ½-inch pieces
1¾ cups sugar
2 tablespoons cornstarch
½ teaspoon ground cinnamon
¼ teaspoon freshly ground nutmeg
1 egg, lightly beaten (optional)

1 egg beaten with 1 tablespoon water

Sweetened whipped cream or crème fraîche (garnish)

For crust: Sift flour and salt into large mixing bowl. Using pastry blender, cut in half the shortening until mixture resembles coarse meal. Add remaining shortening and continue to blend until mixture resembles tiny peas. Sprinkle ice water over dough, 1 tablespoon at a time, mixing with fork until soft ball forms. Shape into ball, cover with waxed paper or foil and chill several hours or overnight. *Dough can also be prepared in food processor using standard method.*

Lightly flour board and roll out half of dough. Press into 9-inch pie pan and trim, leaving a 1-inch overhang. Reserve remaining half of pastry.

For filling: Place rack in lower third of oven and preheat to 400°F. Combine strawberries and rhubarb in large mixing bowl. Mix together sugar, cornstarch, cinnamon and nutmeg and sprinkle over fruit, tossing gently to blend. Add egg and toss again. Spoon mixture into bottom curst.

Roll out remaining pastry on lightly floured board and cut into ½-inch strips, using pastry wheel if possible to make a more decorative lattice. Lay half the pastry strips horizontally 1 inch apart over filled pie. Weave the first vertical cross strip through center of pie, gently folding back corresponding portion of horizontal strips as you work over and under; *do not press down firmly.* Repeat, working outward from center to both sides, and placing cross strips about 1 inch apart, until lattice is completed. Trim any overhanging strips to rim of pie pan.

Fold overhang of lower crust over strips and press firmly around edges to seal. Brush with egg and water to glaze. Bake 40 to 45 minutes, or until crust is golden. Serve warm or at room temperature garnished with sweetened whipped cream or crème fraîche.

For leaf decoration: Roll remaining half of pastry ⅛ to ¼ inch thick. Using leaf canapé cutter, make about 2 dozen leaves. "Etch" veins with dull side of knife. Use remaining pastry as needed to form flower shape. Brush egg-water glaze on outer rim of pie shell. Place leaves around rim, pressing lightly but firmly. Transfer flower to center of filling. Brush pastry with additional glaze and bake as directed.

Fresh Plum Tart with Whipped Cream

A German specialty that is best served the same day as baked.

8 to 10 servings

Cookie Crust Pastry
2 cups all purpose flour
½ cup plus 2 tablespoons sugar
⅛ teaspoon salt
¾ cup (1½ sticks) well-chilled unsalted butter, cut into 1-inch pieces
3 egg yolks
1 teaspoon vanilla
½ cup ground blanched almonds
2 teaspoons grated lemon peel

4 pounds ripe firm-fleshed plums

½ cup finely ground blanched almonds
2 teaspoons sugar

Streusel
1 cup all purpose flour
⅔ cup sugar
½ cup ground blanched almonds
1½ tablespoons grated lemon peel
½ cup (1 stick) chilled unsalted butter, cut into ½-inch pieces

2 cups whipping cream
2 tablespoons slivovitz or other plum brandy (optional)

For pastry: Mix flour, sugar and salt in large bowl. Cut in butter until mixture resembles coarse meal. Blend in yolks one at a time, adding vanilla with last yolk. Mix in ground almonds and lemon peel. Gather dough into ball; flatten into disc. Wrap in plastic and chill at least 1 hour or overnight.

Slice plums vertically on one side only and remove pits. Set plums aside.

Roll dough out on lightly floured chilled surface into 12- to 13-inch circle ¼ inch thick, working quickly and flouring dough lightly as necessary to prevent sticking. Transfer to 10-inch springform pan, pressing halfway up sides. Use dough scraps to repair cracks. Refrigerate dough 20 minutes.

Position rack in lower part of oven and preheat to 425°F. Mix ½ cup ground almonds and 2 teaspoons sugar. Spread over pastry. Starting at edge of pastry, stand plums tightly together upright in concentric circles. Set last plums upright in center.

For streusel: Blend flour, sugar, almonds and lemon peel in large bowl. Cut in butter until mixture is crumbly. (*Can be prepared 1 day ahead, covered and refrigerated.*) Sprinkle over plums; layer will be thick.

Bake tart 15 minutes. Reduce oven temperature to 400°F. Reposition rack in center of oven. Continue baking tart until streusel is golden brown and plums have released some juice, 30 to 45 minutes. Cool tart in pan 15 minutes. Gently unbuckle springform *but do not remove*. Let stand 25 minutes. Remove springform. Cool completely.

Just before serving, beat cream in medium bowl until soft peaks form. Add plum brandy if desired and continue beating until soft mounds form; do not whip until stiff. Cut tart into wedges and top with whipped cream.

Peaches and Cream Pie

6 to 8 servings

1 unbaked 9-inch pie shell

¾ cup sugar
¼ cup all purpose flour
¼ teaspoon salt
¼ teaspoon freshly grated nutmeg

¼ teaspoon cinnamon
3 cups peeled sliced peaches (about 5 medium)
1 cup whipping cream
Whipped cream (garnish)

Preheat oven to 350°F. Prick pie shell with fork. Bake 10 minutes. Set aside to cool. Increase oven temperature to 400°F.

Combine sugar, flour, salt, nutmeg and cinnamon in large bowl. Add peaches and toss gently. Spoon mixture into pie shell. Pour whipping cream over top. Bake until set, about 40 to 45 minutes. Let cool to room temperature. Serve with whipped cream.

Favorite Fresh Peach Pie

8 servings

Crust
2 cups sifted unbleached all purpose flour
¾ teaspoon salt
½ cup (1 stick) well-chilled unsalted butter
¼ cup solid vegetable shortening
1 tablespoon grated lemon peel
¼ cup well-chilled peach nectar
1 to 2 tablespoons fresh lemon juice

Glaze
1¼ cups peach nectar
½ cup plus 2 tablespoons peach jam
2 tablespoons dark rum

Filling
½ to ¾ cup sugar (depending on sweetness of peaches)
¼ cup firmly packed brown sugar
3 to 3½ tablespoons cornstarch
8 medium peaches (about 2¼ pounds)
2 tablespoons fresh lemon juice
¼ teaspoon cinnamon
⅛ teaspoon freshly grated nutmeg
⅛ teaspoon salt

1 egg beaten with 2 teaspoons water

For crust: Combine flour and salt in large bowl. Cut in butter and shortening with pastry blender or 2 knives until mixture resembles coarse meal. Sprinkle with lemon peel and toss lightly. Gradually add chilled peach nectar, blending gently but thoroughly. Add enough lemon juice to make firm dough. Form dough into ball, then flatten into disc. Cover with plastic wrap and refrigerate for at least 30 minutes.

For glaze: Combine all ingredients in small saucepan and stir to blend. Cook over medium heat until reduced to about ¾ cup, about 45 minutes. Strain and cool slightly.

For filling: Combine sugars and cornstarch in small bowl and mix well. Transfer some of sugar mixture to large bowl. To facilitate peeling peaches, immerse 4 at a time in boiling water for 2 minutes. Drain and run under cold water. Peel and cut into ¼- to ½-inch slices. Arrange layer of slices on top of sugar mixture in large bowl. Repeat layers with remaining sugar mixture and peach slices. Toss gently to blend. Sprinkle with lemon juice, spices and salt and toss again, blending thoroughly.

To assemble: Position rack in lower third of oven and preheat to 425°F. Roll dough out on lightly floured surface to circle ¼ inch thick. Roll up on rolling pin and unroll over 9-inch metal pie pan. Press dough gently into place without stretching. Trim edge, leaving ½-inch overhang (reserve trimmings). Brush bottom and sides of pastry with glaze. Layer filling neatly in pastry.

Gather dough trimmings together and roll out into circle ¼ inch thick. Cut ½-inch-wide strips of dough. Arrange in lattice design atop filling, pressing ends into edge of crust. Fold pastry overhang up over lattice ends and crimp decoratively. Carefully brush lattice and crimped edge with beaten egg mixture. Cut strip of foil 2 to 3 inches wide and about 30 inches long and cover edge of crust. Bake 20 minutes. Remove foil and continue baking until golden, about 20 to 30 minutes. Transfer pie to rack and let cool slightly. Serve warm.

Fresh Peach Tart (Tarte aux Pêches)

This is best served within two hours of assembly.

8 servings

Pâte Brisée Sucrée
1½ cups all purpose flour
  1 tablespoon sugar
    Pinch of salt
  ½ cup (1 stick) well-chilled unsalted butter, cut into small pieces
  2 to 3 tablespoons ice cold orange juice
  1 teaspoon vanilla

Crème Pâtissière
  1 cup milk
  ½ cup sugar
  ¼ cup all purpose flour
  3 egg yolks
  1 tablespoon unsalted butter
  3 tablespoons finely ground toasted almonds

  1 quart (4 cups) water
  ¼ cup fresh lemon juice
  4 ripe medium peaches

Glaze
  ⅔ cup peach or apricot jam
  2 tablespoons amaretto

For pâte: Combine flour, sugar and salt in large bowl. Cut in butter with pastry blender until mixture resembles coarse meal. Combine orange juice and vanilla in small bowl. Add to flour mixture 1 tablespoon at a time, blending until dough just holds together and can be shaped into ball (if weather is hot and humid, less liquid may be required). Flatten dough into disc. Wrap in plastic and refrigerate about 10 minutes.

Place dough between 2 sheets of waxed paper and roll into 12-inch circle ⅛ inch thick (if dough appears sticky, return to refrigerator for 5 minutes). Remove top piece of waxed paper and invert dough into 10-inch tart pan with removable bottom. Remove remaining piece of waxed paper. Press dough into bottom and sides of pan; trim excess, allowing ½-inch overlap. Fold excess inside to form double thickness on sides and press firmly. Prick bottom and sides of pastry with fork. Cover with plastic wrap and refrigerate until firm, about 1 hour (or freeze for 30 minutes).

Position rack in center of oven and preheat to 400°F. Set tart pan on baking sheet. Line pastry with waxed paper and fill with rice or dried beans. Bake 8 to 10 minutes. Remove waxed paper and rice or beans. Prick bottom of shell again and continue baking until lightly browned, about 8 minutes. Remove tart shell from oven and let cool.

For crème pâtissière: Combine milk, sugar, flour and egg yolks in processor or blender and mix well. Transfer to small saucepan. Cook over low heat until custard has thickened, about 3 minutes. Remove from heat and stir in butter. Mix in almonds, blending well. Cover with plastic wrap and refrigerate.

Combine water and lemon juice in large bowl and set aside. Combine peaches in large saucepan with enough water to cover and bring to boil over high heat. Let boil 20 to 30 seconds. Remove peaches from saucepan using slotted spoon and plunge into ice water to stop cooking process. Drain peaches well; peel off skins. Cut fruit in half and discard pits. Slice peaches into wedges ¼ inch thick. Add to acidulated water to prevent discoloration. Set aside.

For glaze: Combine jam and liqueur in processor or blender and puree. Lightly brush inside of tart shell with glaze.

Spoon crème pâtissière into shell. Drain peaches thoroughly and pat dry with paper towel. Arrange peaches in concentric circles over pastry cream. Brush lightly with glaze. Refrigerate. Serve tart at room temperature.

Piedmontese Gingered Pear Pie

This unusual dessert should be served warm, with crème fraîche, preferably within 6 hours of baking (the pie tends to become soggy after that time). Drop the pears into lemon water as they are sliced to prevent discoloration.

6 to 8 servings

³/₄ cup dry red wine
³/₄ cup sugar
2 to 2¹/₂ tablespoons minced candied ginger
¹/₂ teaspoon finely grated lemon zest (peel)
10 firm, unblemished pears (Bosc, Seckel or Bartlett), peeled, cored and cut into 1-inch chunks

2 twists freshly ground black pepper

Sweet Cornmeal Pastry*

Combine wine, sugar, ginger and zest in large saucepan over medium-high heat. Bring to boil, stirring constantly until sugar is dissolved. Add pears and continue cooking until slightly softened, about 5 minutes. Remove from heat and let cool in wine mixture. Drain well in colander. Season with pepper.

Grease 8-inch square glass baking dish. Pat ²/₃ of pastry evenly into dish, dipping hands under water and shaking off excess moisture if dough seems too sticky. Refrigerate for 30 minutes.

Position rack in lower third of oven and preheat to 400°F. Spoon pears into pastry. Roll out remaining pastry on floured surface and place over fruit. Seal edges and make several slashes in crust. Bake for 15 minutes. Reduce oven to 375°F and bake until pastry is crisp, about 30 minutes. Serve either warm or at room temperature.

*Sweet Cornmeal Crust

1¹/₄ cups unbleached all purpose flour
¹/₂ cup sugar
¹/₃ cup yellow cornmeal
¹/₈ teaspoon salt

¹/₂ cup (1 stick) well-chilled unsalted butter
1 egg, beaten to blend
2 tablespoons (about) cold water

Combine flour, sugar, cornmeal and salt in large bowl. Cut in butter with pastry blender until coarse meal forms. Add egg and cold water, tossing with a fork until dough is just moistened and can be gathered into a loose ball. Wrap dough in waxed paper and refrigerate at least 2 hours.

Pear Tart

2 servings

Crust
1 cup all purpose flour
2 teaspoons sugar
¹/₄ teaspoon salt
5 tablespoons unsalted butter, cut into pieces
2 to 3 tablespoons ice water

Pastry Cream
2 tablespoons sugar
1 egg yolk
1 tablespoon all purpose flour
¹/₂ cup milk
1 ¹/₂-inch piece vanilla bean

Filling
1 cup sugar
¹/₂ cup water
2 firm pears, peeled, cored and thinly sliced

Glaze
¹/₄ cup raspberry or apricot jam

1 tablespoon grated walnuts

For crust: Combine flour, sugar and salt in medium bowl. Cut in butter using pastry blender or 2 knives until mixture resembles coarse meal. Sprinkle water over mixture and blend with fork until dough forms ball. Wrap in plastic and refrigerate at least 1 hour.

Preheat oven to 350°F. Roll dough out on lightly floured surface into 8 × 11-inch rectangle. Trim edges evenly. Transfer to baking sheet. Trim ¾-inch strips off each side. Lightly moisten 1 inch along outer edges of rectangle. Set dough strips along edges to form double thickness, moistening with water so strips adhere. Trim. Crimp with fork. Thoroughly prick center of tart with fork. Bake until golden brown, about 30 minutes. Let cool.

For cream: Whisk sugar and egg yolk in small bowl until thick and creamy. Gradually blend in flour. Combine milk and vanilla bean in small saucepan and bring to boil over medium-high heat. Pour milk into sugar mixture in thin steady stream, stirring with wooden spoon. Strain into saucepan and bring to boil over low heat, whisking constantly. Continue cooking until very thick, 10 minutes. Remove from heat and let cool completely.

For filling: Combine sugar and water in medium skillet and bring to boil over medium-high heat. Let boil 10 minutes. Reduce heat to low, add pears and cook until tender, about 5 minutes. Drain pears well; let cool.

For glaze: Melt jam in small saucepan over medium heat. Strain through cheesecloth into small bowl.

To assemble: Spoon cream into pastry shell, spreading evenly. Arrange pears in single layer over cream. Brush jam over pears. Sprinkle with nuts and serve.

Swiss Plum Tart

Mango can be substituted for plums.

8 servings

Sweet Spice Short Pastry
- 2 cups whole wheat pastry flour
- 2 tablespoons finely ground almonds or almond paste
- 1 teaspoon cinnamon
- ½ teaspoon ground ginger
  Finely grated peel of 1 lemon
- 10 tablespoons (1¼ sticks) well-chilled unsalted butter, cut into ½-inch pieces
- 2 tablespoons light honey
- 2 tablespoons (or more) ice water

  Additional whole wheat pastry flour
- 1 egg, beaten to blend

- 2 tablespoons dry whole wheat breadcrumbs

Filling
- 1 to 1½ pounds fresh sweet plums (Italian prune or greengage), pitted and quartered
- ½ cup finely chopped walnuts or pecans
- ¼ cup light honey
- ¼ cup honey-sweetened currant jelly*

For pastry: Combine flour, ground almonds, cinnamon, ginger and lemon peel in large mixing bowl. Add butter and blend with fingertips until mixture resembles coarse meal. Combine honey and 2 tablespoons water in small bowl. Add to flour mixture and blend well, adding more water 1 tablespoon at a time if dough is too dry. Turn dough out onto unfloured work surface and quickly form into ball. Cover with plastic; chill 30 minutes.

Cut 2 pieces of waxed paper 24 inches long. Place 1 sheet on work surface and dust with additional flour. Wrap ⅓ of dough in plastic wrap and return to refrigerator. Set remaining dough in center of waxed paper and sprinkle with flour. Flatten dough with rolling pin and cover with remaining sheet of waxed paper. Roll dough out to thickness of ⅛ inch. Remove top sheet of waxed paper. Lifting bottom sheet, invert dough into 8-inch pie pan. Press dough firmly against sides and bottom of pan. Trim excess, allowing 1-inch overlap. Turn overlap under and flute. Brush edge with some of beaten egg. Prick bottom and sides with fork.

Preheat oven to 350°F. Line pastry with waxed paper and fill with dried beans or rice. Bake 25 minutes. Discard paper and beans or rice. Sprinkle bread-crumbs over bottom of shell.

For filling: Combine plums, ¼ cup chopped nuts, honey and currant jelly in large bowl and mix gently with wooden spoon. Turn into pastry shell.

Preheat oven to 350°F. Roll remaining dough out between 2 sheets of floured waxed paper. Cut dough into ½-inch-wide strip, about 9 to 10 inches long. Arrange strips in lattice pattern over top of tart. Press strips against rim of pastry, pinching off excess. Brush top of pastry with beaten egg and sprinkle with remaining chopped nuts. Bake until filling is bubbly and top is golden, about 30 to 35 minutes.

*If using green or yellow plums, substitute honey-sweetened apricot jam for jelly.

Deep-Dish Plum Pie

Before measuring flour and cornmeal for this recipe, sift into dry measuring cups and sweep tops level.

6 to 8 servings

4 pounds slightly underripe red plums, pitted and sliced into eighths
1½ cups sugar
⅓ cup plus 2 tablespoons all purpose flour
Finely grated peel (colored part only) of 1 small orange

1½ cups sifted unbleached all purpose flour
½ cup sifted stone-ground yellow cornmeal

2 tablespoons sugar
¼ teaspoon salt
5 tablespoons well-chilled unsalted butter, cut into pieces
3 tablespoons well-chilled solid vegetable shortening
3 tablespoons whipping cream

1 egg yolk beaten with 1 tablespoon water (glaze)
Vanilla ice cream

Combine plums, 1½ cups sugar, ⅓ cup plus 2 tablespoons flour and orange peel. Let mixture stand 30 minutes, stirring occasionally.

Blend 1½ cups flour, cornmeal, 2 tablespoons sugar and salt in processor 1 to 2 seconds. Add butter and shortening and mix until coarse meal forms, about 10 seconds. With machine running, add cream through feed tube 1 tablespoon at a time. Turn dough out onto lightly floured surface. With heel of hand, push small pieces of dough down onto surface away from you to blend butter and flour thoroughly. Gather dough into ball. Wrap in plastic. Refrigerate at least 20 minutes.

Preheat oven to 375°F. Lightly butter 1½-quart baking dish about 3 inches deep. Pour plum mixture into dish. Bake until bubbly, about 25 minutes.

Roll dough out on lightly floured surface to thickness of ⅜ inch. Cut out rounds using 2½-inch cutter. Using spatula, arrange rounds atop hot plums, overlapping slightly and leaving ½-inch border of filling around edge of dish. Brush dough with glaze. Bake pie until crust is golden brown and juices are thick, 30 to 35 minutes. Serve warm or at room temperature with vanilla ice cream.

Plum-Almond Tart

8 servings

Almond Crust
2¼ **cups ground toasted almonds**
¾ **cup (1½ sticks) unsalted butter, melted**
⅓ **cup sugar**

Almond Filling
1 **pound small red or purple plums, halved and pitted**

1½ **cups whipping cream**
½ **cup sugar**
⅓ **cup amaretto**
2 **eggs**
2 **egg yolks**

For crust: Preheat oven to 375°F. Butter 10-inch tart pan. Combine almonds, butter and sugar in small bowl and mix well. Set aside ⅔ cup crumbs; press remainder onto bottom and sides of tart pan. Bake 10 minutes. Retain oven temperature at 375°F.

For filling: Arrange plums cut side down in crust. Mix cream, sugar, liqueur, eggs and yolks and pour over fruit. Sprinkle reserved crumbs between plums. Bake until custard is just set, about 30 minutes. Serve tart warm.

Crust can be baked 1 day ahead, wrapped loosely and kept at room temperature until filling is prepared.

Tomato-Orange Tart (Mortarete)

Underripe tomatoes are transformed into a special dessert in this recipe from Sciacca, a small Sicilian town.

6 servings

Tomato Preserves
2¼ **pounds firm underripe (green or pale red) tomatoes**
1¾ **cups sugar**

Eggless Crust
1⅔ **cups all purpose flour**
¼ **cup sugar**
½ **teaspoon baking powder**
6 **tablespoons (¾ stick) well-chilled butter**

1 **teaspoon thinly sliced orange peel (colored part only)**
3½ **tablespoons (about) dry Marsala or medium-dry Sherry**

1 **teaspoon thinly sliced orange peel (colored part only)**
½ **cup shelled raw unsalted pistachio nuts, ground**
2 **oranges**

For preserves: Peel tomatoes using sharp knife or vegetable peeler. Cut in half and squeeze out seeds. Cut tomatoes into ¼-inch cubes. Combine with sugar in heavy large saucepan over low heat. Cover and cook 20 minutes, stirring occasionally. Uncover and simmer until liquid is consistency of heavy syrup, stirring frequently near end of cooking time, about 1½ hours. Cool. (*Can be prepared 3 weeks ahead. Cover and refrigerate.*)

For crust: Combine flour, sugar and baking powder in medium bowl. Cut in butter until coarse meal forms. Mix in 1 teaspoon orange peel. Sprinkle with enough Marsala to moisten dough, tossing until mixture starts to gather together. Knead just until dough binds together. (*Can be prepared up to 3 days ahead and refrigerated.*)

Preheat oven to 375°F. Grease 7 × 10½- to 12-inch oval baking dish and dust with flour. Roll dough out between sheets of waxed paper to scant ¼-inch-thick oval. Transfer to prepared dish, removing paper. Press dough into dish. Trim to height of 1½ inches. Stir 1 teaspoon orange peel into tomato preserves and spread in tart. Sprinkle nuts evenly over top. Cut peel and all white pith from oranges. Halve lengthwise, then cut crosswise into ¼-inch-thick slices. Discard any seeds. Arrange oranges atop nuts. Fold over pastry edges. Bake until crust is golden brown, about 45 minutes. Cool on rack. Serve at room temperature.

Maid-of-Honor Pie

6 to 8 servings

1 9-ounce jar seedless raspberry jam
1 unbaked 9-inch pie crust
¼ cup (½ stick) butter, room temperature
3 tablespoons sugar
1 egg

½ cup sifted all purpose flour
¼ teaspoon baking powder
Pinch of salt
1½ teaspoons milk
1 teaspoon almond extract
1 cup dried currants
Vanilla ice cream

Preheat oven to 400°F. Spread jam evenly over bottom of pie shell. Combine butter, sugar and egg in medium bowl and beat until fluffy. Sift flour, baking powder and salt into egg mixture. Stir in milk and almond extract. Blend in currants. Drop batter by spoonfuls over jam, spreading evenly. Bake until top is browned, about 30 minutes. Serve pie warm with vanilla ice cream.

Apricot and Almond Tarts (Mirlitons de Rouen)

Makes 12 tarts

Janine's Pâte Brisée*
½ cup blanched almonds
½ cup sugar
1 egg, beaten to blend
¾ cup apricot jam (preferably homemade)

1 or 2 teaspoons apricot brandy or Cognac
Sliced almonds and powdered sugar (garnish)

Prepare pastry. Wrap and chill thoroughly (allow 10 to 15 minutes in freezer or about 1 hour in refrigerator).

Butter tartlet molds. Preheat oven to 400°F. Roll chilled pastry ⅛ inch thick. Cut and fit neatly into molds.

Finely grind almonds in food processor or by hand. Add sugar and egg and beat well. Place 1 teaspoon of jam in each tartlet and cover with almond mixture, filling just ½ full. Bake 20 minutes.

Meanwhile, puree remaining ½ cup apricot jam with brandy to taste in blender. Brush lightly over baked pastries and garnish with almonds. Cool on wire rack. Dust generously with powdered sugar just before serving.

*Janine's Pâte Brisée

1⅔ cups all purpose flour
½ cup (1 stick) butter
1 tablespoon shortening

Pinch of salt
⅓ cup ice water

Combine all ingredients in food processor and mix lightly to form pliable dough, or, if making by hand, combine flour and salt in mixing bowl. Cut in butter and shortening and blend until mixture resembles coarse meal. Add water a little at a time and gather mixture gently into ball. Shape into 8-inch circle, wrap in plastic and chill.

Sweet Fruit Tart (Canestrelletti)

This versatile pastry dough can also be rolled and cut into shortbread-type cookies.

12 servings

1 cup (2 sticks) unsalted butter, room temperature
1 cup sugar
2 cups sifted all purpose flour
4 egg yolks
¼ teaspoon vanilla

Finely grated peel of 1 lemon
Pinch of salt

Jam, thick marmalade or sliced fresh fruit
1 egg

Cream butter with sugar until smooth. Beat in flour alternately with yolks, blending well after each addition. Stir in vanilla, lemon peel and salt and mix thoroughly (dough will be stiff). Form dough into ball; wrap in plastic and flatten into disc. Chill 30 minutes.

Preheat oven to 325°F. Roll dough out on lightly floured board to thickness of ¼ inch. Transfer to 8- or 9-inch glass pie dish. Trim overlap to ½ inch and fold under; pinch to form rim. Add thin layer of jam, marmalade or fruit. Roll pastry scraps ¼ inch thick. Cut into 6 to 8 strips each ½ inch wide. Arrange over top of tart in lattice pattern, crimping to edges. Beat egg and use to glaze pastry. Bake until tart is golden, about 45 minutes. Let cool completely, then loosen from dish with knife and transfer to serving plate. *Can be made several days ahead.*

Pasta Fleura

This simple pastry is perfect with coffee or tea. For a variation, spread half the pastry with cherry preserves and half with apricot preserves.

Makes about 50

¼ cup lukewarm water (95°F)
1 yeast cake
1½ cups (3 sticks) well-chilled unsalted butter
4 cups bleached all purpose flour

4 egg yolks
¼ cup milk

2 pounds cherry preserves
1 egg, beaten to blend (glaze)

Preheat oven to 350°F. Grease 11 × 16-inch baking pan. Combine water and yeast in small bowl; stir to dissolve. Cut butter into flour in processor until coarse meal forms. (If using standard-size processor, mix dough in 2 batches.) Add yeast, yolks and milk and process until ball forms.

Roll ⅔ of dough out on lightly floured surface to 3/16-inch-thick rectangle. Transfer to prepared pan; trim edges. Spread with preserves. Roll remaining dough out on lightly floured surface to 3/16-inch-thick rectangle. Cut into ¾-inch-wide strips. Arrange in lattice pattern atop preserves. Crimp edges to seal. Carefully brush lattice with glaze. Bake until pastry is golden brown, about 40 minutes. Cool. (*Can be prepared ahead. Wrap tightly and refrigerate 5 days or freeze 1 month. Bring to room temperature before serving.*) Cut into 2-inch squares.

🍎 *Dried Fruit*

Tarte d'Abricots

6 to 8 servings

Filling
1 pound dried apricots
1 cup (or more) water
1 cup sugar

Crust
1 cup (2 sticks) unsalted butter,
   room temperature
1 cup sugar

2 egg yolks
1 cup ground almonds
1 teaspoon vanilla
   Pinch of cinnamon
2 cups sifted all purpose flour

1 egg white, beaten to blend

For filling: Combine apricots, 1 cup water and sugar in medium saucepan over medium-high heat and cook until tender, stirring occasionally and adding more water if necessary. Transfer to processor or blender and puree. Return to pan and set aside.

For crust: Position rack in center of oven and preheat to 350°F. Cream butter with sugar in medium bowl until smooth. Add egg yolks, almonds, vanilla and cinnamon, mixing well after each addition. Gradually blend in flour and work with hands until dough is smoothly blended.

Divide dough in half. Press half onto bottom and sides of 9-inch springform pan. Pour apricot mixture into pan, spreading evenly. Pat remaining pastry out into rectangle. Cut into 1-inch-wide strips. Arrange in lattice pattern over filling. Brush strips with egg white. Bake until top is golden, about 45 minutes. Transfer to rack and let cool completely. Just before serving, remove springform and transfer tart to platter.

Winter Fruit Pie

A perfect ending to a cold-weather dinner. Also wonderful at brunch or with coffee.

8 to 10 servings

Hazelnut Crust
1 cup hazelnuts, toasted and
   husked
1/4 cup sugar
1 cup all purpose flour
1/4 teaspoon cinnamon
1/8 teaspoon salt
7 tablespoons unsalted butter,
   room temperature
1 egg yolk, room temperature

Fruit Filling
1 12-ounce package pitted prunes,
   finely chopped

1 6-ounce package dried apricots,
   finely chopped
3/4 cup dry white wine, preferably
   Italian
2/3 cup honey
1/4 cup Grand Marnier
1 teaspoon grated lemon peel

1 hazelnut, toasted and husked
2 tablespoons toasted pine nuts

For crust: Grease 9-inch round fluted tart pan with removable bottom. Finely chop hazelnuts with sugar in processor. Add flour, cinnamon and salt and blend using 3 on/off turns. Add butter and yolk and mix until dough begins to gather together. Press dough into prepared pan, making sides 1/2 inch thick. Pierce bottom with fork. Refrigerate at least 30 minutes.

Preheat oven to 350°F. Bake crust until pale golden, 25 to 30 minutes.

For filling: Combine prunes, apricots, wine and honey in heavy small saucepan. Cover and simmer until all liquid is absorbed, stirring occasionally, 15 to 20 minutes. Cool 5 minutes. Mix in Grand Marnier and lemon peel.

Pour filling into crust. (*Can be prepared 1 day ahead.*) Garnish with nuts. Serve warm or at room temperature.

Lemon-Raisin Tart

8 to 10 servings

1 **pound golden raisins**
6 **small unblemished lemons, thinly sliced**

½ **cup (1 stick) unsalted butter**

1 **cup sugar**

Pastry
1⅓ **cups all purpose flour**
1 **tablespoon firmly packed dark brown sugar**

½ **teaspoon salt**
½ **cup (1 stick) well-chilled unsalted butter, cut into pieces**
¼ **cup ice water**

Sweetened whipped cream flavored with vanilla

Place raisins in 2-quart saucepan. Cover with cold water and bring to boil. Remove from heat and let stand 30 minutes. Drain well, reserving liquid. Combine liquid with lemon slices; bring to boil over medium heat and boil 2 minutes. Remove from heat and let stand 30 minutes. Drain well.

Use ¼ cup butter to generously coat bottom of deep 10-inch tart pan. Melt remaining ¼ cup butter in small cup set in pan of simmering water.

Sprinkle ⅓ cup sugar over bottom of tart pan. Arrange ⅓ of lemon slices over. Cover with ⅓ of raisins. Drizzle ⅓ of melted butter evenly over top. Repeat layering twice more. Set aside.

For pastry: Preheat oven to 375°F. Combine flour, brown sugar and salt in large bowl and blend well. Using fingertips, work in butter until mixture is consistency of coarse crumbs. Sprinkle with water and form into ball, kneading gently. Place on floured surface and pat into 11-inch circle, turning dough over once or twice.

Set dough over fruit, pressing gently but firmly; tuck excess pastry into sides. Prick pastry in several places with point of knife to allow steam to escape. Bake 2 hours (if pastry browns too quickly, cover with piece of foil).

Set serving plate on top of tart; invert, remove pan and let stand at least 1 hour. Serve with whipped cream.

Regal Raisin Date Pie

6 to 8 servings

1 unbaked 9-inch deep-dish
   pie crust

½ cup (1 stick) butter, room
   temperature
1½ cups firmly packed brown sugar
4 egg yolks
2 tablespoons all purpose flour
1 tablespoon fresh lemon juice
1 teaspoon cinnamon
1 teaspoon vanilla

½ teaspoon freshly grated nutmeg
1 cup half and half
1 cup coarsely chopped pecans
¾ cup chopped dates
¾ cup chopped raisins
1 cup whipping cream, whipped
2 tablespoons powdered sugar
   Pinch of cinnamon

Preheat oven to 375°F. Bake pie shell 5 minutes and set aside. Reduce oven temperature to 350°F.

Cream butter with brown sugar in large bowl until light and fluffy. Beat in egg yolks, flour, lemon juice, 1 teaspoon cinnamon, vanilla and nutmeg. Stir in half and half, blending well. Add pecans, dates and raisins. Pour mixture into pie shell. Bake until knife inserted near center comes out clean, about 45 to 50 minutes (cover crust with foil if edges begin browning too quickly). Let cool. To serve, combine whipped cream, powdered sugar and cinnamon in small bowl. Pipe rosettes of whipped cream mixture around edge of pie or pass separately.

Hazelnut-Fig Pastry

12 servings

Hazelnut Crust
2 cups sifted unbleached all
   purpose flour
1 cup sugar
1 tablespoon baking powder
¼ teaspoon ground cloves
¼ teaspoon salt
1 cup (2 sticks) well-chilled
   unsalted butter
1½ cups hazelnuts, toasted, partially
   husked and finely ground
2 egg yolks
1 egg
1½ tablespoon grated orange peel
1 teaspoon vanilla
½ teaspoon almond extract

Fig-Marsala Filling
1 teaspoon whole cloves
1 pound soft-pack Calimyrna figs,
   quartered
1½ cups Marsala
¾ cup sugar
3 orange slices
2 lemon slices
1 3-inch cinnamon stick
   Pinch of salt

1 egg, beaten to blend (glaze)

For crust: Sift first 5 ingredients into large bowl. Cut in butter until coarse meal forms. Mix in hazelnuts. Make well in center. Add yolks, egg, orange peel, vanilla and almond extract to well and blend with fork. Gradually draw dry ingredients from inner edge of well into center until incorporated. Gather into ball. Cut off ⅔ of dough. Form each piece into round; flatten into discs. Wrap in plastic. Refrigerate 2 hours (*Can be prepared 1 day ahead.*)

For filling: Wrap cloves in single thickness of cheesecloth. Combine with all remaining ingredients except glaze in heavy medium saucepan over low heat. Bring to simmer, stirring until sugar dissolves. Cover and simmer gently until figs are tender, stirring occasionally, about 50 minutes. Let mixture stand for 2 hours.

Discard cloves, orange and lemon slices and cinnamon stick. Transfer figs and cooking liquid to processor and chop finely; do not puree.

Butter 11-inch tart pan with removable bottom. Dust with flour. Roll larger disc of dough out between sheets of waxed paper to ¼-inch-thick round. Transfer to prepared pan, discarding paper. Trim edges. Spread filling in shell. Roll remaining dough out between sheets of waxed paper to ⅜-inch-thick round. Cut into ¾-inch-wide strips (if dough is too soft, refrigerate briefly). Arrange strips atop tart in lattice pattern, spacing 1 inch apart. Trim ends of strips; press strips into shell edges. Chill tart 30 minutes.

Position rack in lower third of oven and preheat to 375°F. Brush lattice with glaze; do not allow to drip onto filling. Bake until center strips are deep brown, covering edges with foil if browning too quickly, about 45 minutes. Cool completely on rack. (*Can be prepared 3 days ahead. Cover tightly and store pastry at room temperature.*)

Ferguson Family's Mincemeat

Originally Pennsylvania Dutch, this recipe yields enough filling for several delicious pies.

Makes about 10¾ cups

3 cups water
1½ pounds beef stew meat, cubed
¾ teaspoon salt

3½ pounds Granny Smith apples, cored and cut into 1-inch pieces
½ medium unpeeled lemon, seeded and cut into ¾-inch pieces
2 cups sugar
1 cup raisins

¾ cup light molasses
½ cup cider vinegar
1¼ teaspoons cinnamon
1¼ teaspoons freshly grated nutmeg
1 teaspoon instant coffee powder
½ teaspoon salt
¼ teaspoon ground cloves

⅓ cup brandy
¼ teaspoon freshly ground pepper

Combine water, beef and salt in heavy large saucepan or Dutch oven over medium-high heat. Bring to boil, skimming foam from surface. Reduce heat, cover and simmer until meat is tender, about 1½ hours.

Remove meat with slotted spoon and cool slightly. Reserve ¾ cup cooking liquid. Coarsely grind meat in batches in processor using on/off turns (or use food grinder). Transfer to another heavy large saucepan or Dutch oven. Coarsely grind apples in batches in processor using on/off turns. Add to meat. Finely grind lemon in processor using on/off turns and add to meat. Mix in reserved liquid and remaining ingredients except brandy and pepper. Simmer over low heat until very thick but not dry, stirring frequently, about 1 hour.

Remove from heat and stir in brandy and pepper. Transfer mincemeat to airtight containers. Cover and cool to room temperature. Refrigerate at least 6 weeks before using.

Prune Tart

The tart can be stored at room temperature several weeks. Pasta frolla, the delicate buttery Italian pastry, has baking powder in it to crisp the crust.

10 to 12 servings

Prune Marmalade
  2 pounds vacuum-packed pitted prunes (about 5 cups)
1¾ cups sugar
1¼ cups water

  1 tablespoon fresh lemon juice
  1 tablespoon vanilla

Pasta Frolla
  2 cups all purpose flour
⅔ cup sugar
  1 tablespoon baking powder
  Pinch of salt
¾ cup (1½ sticks) well-chilled unsalted butter, chopped
  2 egg yolks
  1 egg
1½ teaspoons grated lemon peel

  1 egg, beaten to blend (glaze)

For marmalade: Cook prunes, sugar and water in heavy large saucepan over low heat until sugar dissolves. Increase heat and bring to boil. Cover, reduce heat and simmer gently until prunes are tender, stirring frequently to prevent sticking, about 45 minutes.

Puree hot prune mixture with lemon juice and vanilla in processor until smooth paste, stopping to scrape down bowl. Cool to room temperature. (*Can be prepared 1 day ahead to this point, covered and stored at room temperature.*)

For Pasta Frolla: Mix flour, sugar, baking powder and salt in large bowl. Add butter and blend with fingertips until mixture resembles coarse meal. Make well in center. Add yolks, egg and lemon peel to well and beat to blend. Gradually incorporate flour, mixing until smooth. Form ⅔ of dough into flat disc; form remainder into flat rectangle. Wrap each in plastic and refrigerate at least 1 hour. (*Can be prepared several days ahead and chilled.*)

Grease and lightly flour 11-inch tart pan, 1 inch deep, with removable bottom. Roll pastry disc out between sheets of waxed paper into circle ¹/₁₆ inch thick. Refrigerate or freeze until firm. Remove top sheet of paper and invert dough into pan. Remove remaining paper. Fit into pan; trim edges. Refrigerate or freeze tart shell until firm.

Spoon prune marmalade into shell, spreading top evenly with spatula. Roll pastry rectangle out between sheets of waxed paper into square ⅛ inch thick. Refrigerate or freeze until firm. Cut dough into ½-inch-wide strips using fluted pastry cutter. Refrigerate or freeze until firm. To form lattice top, arrange half of strips diagonally across top of tart, spacing about ¾ inch apart. Arrange remaining strips diagonally in opposite direction, spacing about ¾ inch apart. Trim strips and press ends into edge of shell. Refrigerate at least 30 minutes.

Preheat oven to 375°F. Brush lattice with glaze. Bake tart until golden brown, about 45 minutes (if top browns too quickly, cover with foil during last 10 minutes). Cool completely. Serve at room temperature.

Strawberry Tart with Beurre Noisette

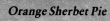

Orange Sherbet Pie

Dick Sharpe

Blue Ribbon Pecan Pie

Chocolate Mousse Pie

Deep-Dish Plum Pie

Caribbean Lime Pie

Coconut-Almond Tart

Top to bottom: Cookie Crust Tart with Boysenberry Puree; Lemon Raspberry Tart; Marzipan Tart

Irwin Horowitz

3 ❧ *Custard and Cream Pies*

"A little slice of heaven" is how any pie or tart in this chapter might be described. The silky fillings, topped by a swirl of whipped cream or a golden meringue peak, literally melt in the mouth. These luscious mixtures are enclosed in a variety of crusts, from the traditional flaky pastry to easy and delicious meringue or crumb layers.

Custard pies have been an American favorite since the Pilgrims picked their first Thanksgiving pumpkins—but the Pilgrims would doubtless be astonished at the refinement of Pumpkin Pie with Candied Orange Peel (page 79). Soothing, creamy Buttermilk Custard Pie (page 60), passed down by generations of Southern bakers, is a wonderful dessert rich in heritage as well as flavor. At the other end of the spectrum, tart Apricot Custard Pie (page 61), with its vividly colored filling and flaky orange-scented crust, is an up-to-the-minute recipe that takes full advantage of the food processor.

For custard pies, an uncooked filling is poured into an unbaked or partially baked crust and then the two are baked together. In the case of cream pies, a prepared filling is added to a fully baked crust; often a meringue topping is added and the pie is returned to the oven until tipped with golden brown. Lemon is one of the most popular filling choices, and the Perfect Lemon Meringue Pie on page 71 is as superlative as its name suggests. For an interesting change, try Burnt Orange Meringue Pie (page 76) or gossamer-light Chef Thomas's Pecan Cream Pie (page 70).

Also included is a selection of cheese pies, every one of which can be made ahead of time. Easy Cherry Cream Cheese Pie (page 80) is assembled in a matter of minutes, while Cheesecake Tart and Wine-glazed Fruit (page 81) is ideal for the most elegant entertaining.

A few preparation hints: When baking a crust without filling, the pastry dough should be fitted loosely into the pie pan and pricked all over with a fork; this will help the crust keep its shape and brown evenly. Pie weights can also be used to maintain a smooth surface. Fillings added at room temperature generally produce the best pies; a hot filling can make the crust soggy, and the extra time required to bake a cold filling may cause the crust to overbake. Adding a meringue? Spread it over the filling all the way to the edge of the crust so that it won't shrink when baked.

Avocado Pie

8 to 10 servings

1 large avocado, peeled, pitted and quartered
1 14-ounce can sweetened condensed milk
¼ cup fresh lemon juice
1 baked 9-inch Graham Cracker Crust,* cooled

1 cup sour cream
2 tablespoons milk
½ cup chopped walnuts

Combine avocado, condensed milk and lemon juice in processor or blender and mix until smooth. Pour mixture into crust.

Combine sour cream and milk in blender or small bowl and mix well. Carefully spread over avocado mixture. Sprinkle with chopped walnuts. Chill thoroughly before serving.

*Graham Cracker Crust

1½ cups graham cracker crumbs (about 20 crackers)

⅓ cup butter, melted
3 tablespoons sugar

Preheat oven to 350°F. Combine all ingredients in large bowl. Turn mixture into 9-inch pie pan, pressing firmly and evenly onto bottom and sides. Bake 10 minutes.

Cranberry Cream Pie

6 to 8 servings

1 12-ounce package fresh cranberries
1¼ cups sugar
1 cup water
2 egg yolks, room temperature
2 tablespoons cornstarch

1 cup sour cream, room temperature
1 baked 9-inch pie crust
1 8-ounce container nondairy whipped topping

Combine cranberries, 1 cup sugar and water in heavy large saucepan. Cook over medium-high heat until very thick, about 10 minutes. Mix yolks, remaining sugar and cornstarch. Add to cranberries. Stir in sour cream and cook until thick, about 4 minutes. Spoon into crust. Refrigerate at least 8 hours or overnight. Just before serving, spoon topping over pie.

Lemon Sponge and Custard Pie

8 servings

1 unbaked 9-inch deep-dish pie shell

1 cup sugar
¼ cup (½ stick) butter, melted
3 tablespoons all purpose flour
1½ cups milk

3 egg yolks, beaten to blend
¼ cup fresh lemon juice
2½ teaspoons freshly grated lemon peel
3 egg whites, room temperature

Position rack in lower third of oven and preheat to 350°F. Line shell with parchment or foil. Fill with dried beans or pie weights. Bake until pastry is set, about 10 minutes. Remove beans and paper. Continue baking 3 minutes. Cool crust.

Increase temperature to 450°F. Blend sugar, butter and flour in large bowl. Add milk, yolks, juice and peel and mix well. Beat egg whites until stiff but not dry. Gently fold ½ cup lemon batter into whites. Fold in remaining batter, being careful not to overmix. Pour into crust. Bake 8 minutes. Reduce temperature to 325°F. Cover edges of crust with foil if browning too quickly. Continue baking until knife inserted in center comes out clean, 25 to 30 minutes. Cool completely on rack. Serve at room temperature.

Sour Cream-Apple Tart

8 to 10 servings

Crust
  1 cup unbleached all purpose flour
  ¼ cup sugar
  ½ cup (1 stick) well-chilled butter
  1 egg
  ½ cup chopped walnuts
  ½ cup apricot jam, heated, strained

Filling
2½ pounds tart apples, peeled, cored and thinly sliced
  1 to 2 teaspoons fresh lemon juice
  3 tablespoons butter
  ¼ cup sugar
  ¼ cup firmly packed brown sugar
  ½ cup raisins
  1 teaspoon cinnamon
  ¾ teaspoon grated lemon peel

Topping
  2 cups sour cream
  ¼ cup whipping cream
  2 eggs
  ¼ cup sugar
  ½ teaspoon vanilla

  Finely chopped walnuts

For crust: Preheat oven to 375°F. Mix flour and sugar in medium bowl. Cut in butter using pastry blender or 2 knives until mixture resembles coarse meal. Blend in egg. Stir in walnuts. Pat dough into bottom and ½ inch up sides of 10-inch springform pan. Bake until golden brown, 20 to 25 minutes. Cool crust. Spread with warm jam.

For filling: Toss apples with lemon juice to taste. Melt butter in heavy large skillet over low heat. Add apples and both sugars and stir to mix. Cover and cook until apples are just tender, 10 to 12 minutes. Uncover, increase heat to medium-high and cook until liquid has evaporated, 7 to 8 minutes. Stir in raisins, cinnamon and peel. Cool.

For topping: Preheat oven to 350°F. Beat sour cream, whipping cream, eggs, sugar and vanilla in bowl.

Spoon filling into crust. Very slowly pour topping over, lifting apples so topping seeps through. Bake until topping is consistency of cooked custard, 35 to 40 minutes. Sprinkle top edge of tart with chopped walnuts. Cool to room temperature. Refrigerate at least 8 hours or overnight. Serve chilled.

Buttermilk Custard Pie

A cheesecake-like custard pie recipe from early Southern kitchens.

12 servings

½ cup all purpose flour
2 tablespoons (¼ stick) butter, room temperature
6 egg yolks
1½ to 2 cups sugar

4 cups (1 quart) buttermilk
2 teaspoons lemon extract
1 12-inch pie crust,* baked and cooled

Position rack in center of oven and preheat to 425°F. Combine flour and butter in medium bowl and mix well. Whisk in yolks, 1½ cups sugar, buttermilk and extract and beat until smooth. Taste and add additional sugar if desired. Pour into prepared pie crust. Bake 10 minutes; reduce heat to 350°F and continue baking until knife inserted between edge and center of filling comes out clean, about 45 to 50 minutes. Cool to room temperature. Chill until serving time.

Pie can be prepared up to 2 days ahead.

*Pie Crust

¾ cup unbleached all purpose flour
⅓ cup cake flour
2 tablespoons sugar
⅛ teaspoon salt

6 tablespoons (¾ stick) well-chilled unsalted butter, cut into small pieces
3 to 4 tablespoons ice water

Combine flours, sugar and salt in processor and mix well. Add butter and blend using on/off turns until mixture resembles coarse meal. Add water and mix using on/off turns just until dough begins to mass together. Gather dough into ball, wrap in plastic and refrigerate 1 to 24 hours. (To mix by hand, combine flours, sugar and salt in bowl. Cut in butter with pastry blender until mixture resembles coarse meal. Add water and toss mixture with fork until moistened. Gather dough into ball, wrap and chill 1 to 24 hours.)

Grease 12-inch pie plate and set aside. Roll dough out on lightly floured surface into large circle. Fit into prepared pie plate and flute edges decoratively. Chill 1 to 8 hours.

Preheat oven to 400°F. Line pastry with foil and weight with dried beans, rice or pie weights. Bake 10 minutes. Discard foil and weights and continue baking until crust is golden brown, about 4 minutes. Cool.

Wild's Sour Cream Pie

4 to 6 servings

2 eggs, room temperature
1 cup sugar
1 cup sour cream
½ cup whipping cream
1½ tablespoons bourbon
1 tablespoon all purpose flour

½ teaspoon cinnamon
½ teaspoon freshly grated nutmeg
Pinch of salt
¾ cup raisins
1 unbaked 9-inch pie crust

Preheat oven to 450°F. Beat eggs with sugar in large bowl of electric mixer until thick and creamy, about 3 to 5 minutes. Add next 7 ingredients and blend thoroughly. Stir in raisins. Pour batter into pie shell. Bake 10 minutes. Reduce oven temperature to 350°F and continue baking until knife inserted in center comes out clean, about 35 minutes. Serve pie warm.

❦

Apricot Custard Pie

8 servings

Orange Pastry
- 1 tablespoon grated orange peel
- 3 tablespoons powdered sugar
- ½ cup (1 stick) well-chilled unsalted butter, cut into 8 pieces
- 5 tablespoons cold water
- 1 egg yolk
- 1½ cups unbleached all purpose flour
- ½ teaspoon salt

Custard
- 9 jumbo dried apricots
- ½ cup sugar
- 4 eggs
- ¾ cup fresh orange juice
- ¼ cup whipping cream
- 1 tablespoon fresh lemon juice
- 1 tablespoon Grand Marnier

Meringue
- 4 egg whites
- 4 tablespoons sugar

For pastry: Finely mince orange peel with sugar in processor fitted with steel knife. Add butter, cold water and yolk and blend using 6 on/off turns, then process continuously 5 seconds. Add flour and salt and mix just until dough begins to come together (do not form ball). Turn dough out and gather into ball. Wrap in plastic; flatten into disc. Refrigerate several hours or overnight.

Butter 9-inch metal pie pan. Roll dough out on lightly floured surface into circle ⅛ inch thick. Fit into pan; trim and crimp edges. Prick bottom and sides with fork. Refrigerate until firm, about 30 minutes.

Position rack in center of oven and preheat to 400°F. Line pie shell with parchment and fill with dried beans, rice or pie weights. Bake 10 minutes. Remove paper and weights. Prick shell again and continue baking until browned, about 12 minutes.

Meanwhile, prepare custard: Finely mince apricots and sugar in processor. Add eggs and mix 1 minute, stopping once to scrape down sides of work bowl. With machine running, pour orange juice, cream, lemon juice and Grand Marnier through feed tube and blend 5 seconds. Pour into hot crust. Reduce oven temperature to 375°F. Bake 10 minutes. Reduce oven temperature to 350°F. Continue baking until custard is just set in center, about 18 minutes, covering edges with foil if browning too quickly. Cool pie to room temperature on wire rack.

For meringue: Position rack in center of oven and preheat to 350°F. Beat whites to soft peaks. Beat in sugar 1 tablespoon at a time. Continue beating until stiff but not dry. Spoon meringue atop pie, spreading to crust to cover custard completely. Bake until meringue is lightly browned, about 10 minutes. Serve pie within 4 hours.

Banana Cream Tarts

2 servings

Pastry
- 6 tablespoons all purpose flour
- 1 tablespoon sugar
- Pinch of salt
- 3 tablespoons well-chilled unsalted butter, cut into ½-inch pieces
- 1 egg yolk, beaten to blend
- 1 teaspoon cold water
- ⅛ teaspoon vanilla

Filling
- 2 tablespoons sugar
- 4 teaspoons all purpose flour
- Pinch of salt
- ⅔ cup milk
- 1 egg yolk
- 1 tablespoon dark rum
- 1 teaspoon butter

- 1 small banana
- ¼ cup whipping cream, whipped
- 2 tablespoons toasted shredded coconut

For pastry: Sift flour, sugar and salt into medium bowl. Cut in butter using pastry blender or 2 knives until mixture resembles coarse meal. Blend yolk, water and vanilla in small bowl. Add to flour and blend with fork until mixture just holds together. Shape dough into ball. Wrap in plastic and refrigerate at least 1 hour.

Lightly grease two 4-inch tart pans with removable bottoms. Divide dough in half. Roll out half on lightly floured surface into 6-inch circle $1/8$ inch thick. Repeat with remaining dough. Fit into pans; trim and crimp edges. Refrigerate until firm.

Preheat oven to 425°F. Line pastry shells with greased parchment paper and fill with dried beans, rice or pie weights. Bake 8 minutes. Remove paper and weights. Prick bottoms of shells with fork in several places. Continue baking until shells are golden brown, 7 to 8 minutes, covering edges with foil if rims brown too quickly.

For filling: Blend sugar, flour and salt in top of double boiler set over gently simmering water. Gradually whisk in milk and continue whisking until thickened, about 15 minutes. Cover and cook 10 minutes, whisking occasionally. Remove from heat. Blend yolk and rum in small bowl. Whisk small amount of milk mixture into yolk, then return to saucepan. Place over gently simmering water and whisk 2 minutes. Remove from heat and stir in 1 teaspoon butter. Cool.

Slice banana and arrange in bottoms of shells. Pour cooled filling over. Refrigerate until firm. Just before serving, pipe cream decoratively over tops. Sprinkle with toasted coconut.

Cracker Pie

A light, creamy filling in a nutted meringue shell.

8 servings

3 egg whites, room temperature
1 teaspoon cream of tartar
1 cup sugar
1 teaspoon vanilla
1 cup chopped pecans
16 saltine crackers, crushed
2 tablespoons pineapple or apricot preserves
1 cup whipping cream, whipped
1 $3^1/2$-ounce package flaked coconut

Preheat oven to 350°F. Beat whites in large bowl of electric mixer until foamy, about 2 minutes. Add cream of tartar and beat until soft peaks form. Add sugar and vanilla and continue beating until whites are stiff but not dry, about 30 seconds. Fold in pecans and crushed crackers. Spoon into 9-inch ovenproof glass pie plate. Bake until lightly golden and crisp, 25 to 30 minutes. Cool completely.

Stir preserves into whipped cream in large bowl. Spread over pie. Sprinkle with coconut. Serve immediately.

Coffee Chiffon Pie

8 servings

1 cup graham cracker crumbs
6 tablespoons ($3/4$ stick) butter, melted
2 tablespoons sugar

$1/2$ cup cold water
2 teaspoons instant coffee powder
1 envelope unflavored gelatin
3 egg yolks
$1/3$ cup sugar

$1/8$ teaspoon salt
$1/3$ cup coffee liqueur
1 tablespoon vanilla

1 cup whipping cream
3 egg whites
$1/4$ cup sugar

Shaved semisweet chocolate

Preheat oven to 375°F. Combine crumbs, butter and sugar in medium bowl and mix well. Press into bottom and sides of 9-inch pie plate. Bake 8 minutes. Set aside to cool.

Meanwhile, combine water and coffee powder in medium saucepan and stir until dissolved. Add gelatin and let stand 5 minutes. Add egg yolks, sugar and salt, whisking until well blended. Cook over low heat, stirring constantly, until gelatin is dissolved and mixture thickens (do not boil). Remove from heat. Stir in liqueur and vanilla. Pour into large bowl. Chill until thickened to consistency of unbeaten egg white, 2 to 3 hours.

Whip cream in medium bowl until peaks hold shape (do not overbeat until stiff). Beat egg whites in large bowl of electric mixer at medium speed until soft peaks form. Gradually add ¼ cup sugar, beating constantly until whites are stiff and glossy. Gently fold egg whites into gelatin mixture, then gently fold in whipped cream. Spoon into prepared pie shell. Refrigerate at least 6 hours before serving. Garnish with shaved semisweet chocolate.

Heidi's Irish Coffee Cream Pie

6 to 8 servings

Crust
1 cup graham cracker crumbs
¼ cup (½ stick) butter, melted

Filling
3 cups whipping cream
½ cup plus 1 tablespoon powdered sugar

6 tablespoons Irish whiskey
6 tablespoons coffee liqueur
¼ cup instant coffee powder dissolved in 2 tablespoons hot water
Shaved chocolate

For crust: Preheat oven to 375°F. Combine crumbs and butter in small bowl. Press into 9-inch pie plate and bake until set, about 8 minutes. Cool completely.

For filling: Combine all ingredients except shaved chocolate and beat at medium speed of electric mixer until mixture holds peaks. Pour all but ½ cup into crust, spreading evenly. Spoon remaining filling into pastry bag fitted with rosette tip and pipe frill around rim. Garnish with shaved chocolate. Refrigerate pie at least 4 hours or overnight. Serve chilled.

Chocolate Angel Pie

8 servings

Meringue Crust
2 egg whites, room temperature
⅛ teaspoon cream of tartar
½ cup sugar
½ teaspoon vanilla
⅛ teaspoon salt

4 ounces semisweet chocolate, broken into pieces

3 tablespoons hot water
1 cup whipping cream, whipped
1 teaspoon vanilla
1 ounce semisweet chocolate, grated

For crust: Preheat oven to 300°F. Butter 9-inch ovenproof glass pie plate. Beat whites and cream of tartar in medium bowl of electric mixer until foamy. Combine sugar, vanilla and salt. Gradually add to whites and continue beating until stiff but not dry. Spread in bottom and up sides of prepared dish. Bake until golden, about 50 minutes.

Melt 4 ounces chocolate with hot water in small saucepan over low heat, stirring occasionally. Cool to room temperature. Fold into whipped cream in large bowl. Stir in vanilla. Spoon into crust, spreading evenly. Sprinkle with grated chocolate. Refrigerate overnight.

Chocolate Mousse Pie

A chocolate cookie crumb crust enriches this easy-to-make but dramatic dessert. It can be prepared ahead and frozen; thaw overnight in the refrigerator.

10 to 12 servings

Crust
3 cups chocolate wafer crumbs
½ cup (1 stick) unsalted butter, melted

Filling
1 pound semisweet chocolate
2 eggs
4 egg yolks

2 cups whipping cream
6 tablespoons powdered sugar
4 egg whites, room temperature

Chocolate Leaves
8 ounces (about) semisweet chocolate
1 tablespoon (scant) solid vegetable shortening
Camellia or other waxy leaves

2 cups whipping cream
Sugar

For crust: Combine crumbs and butter. Press on bottom and completely up sides of 10-inch springform pan. Refrigerate 30 minutes (or chill in freezer).

For filling: Soften chocolate in top of double boiler over simmering water. Let cool to lukewarm (95°F). Add whole eggs and mix well. Add yolks and mix until thoroughly blended.

Whip cream with powdered sugar until soft peaks form. Beat egg whites until stiff but not dry. Stir a little of the cream and whites into chocolate mixture to lighten. Fold in remaining cream and whites until completely incorporated. Turn into crust and chill at least 6 hours, preferably overnight.

For leaves: Melt chocolate with shortening in top of double boiler. Using spoon, generously coat underside of leaves. Chill or freeze until firm.

Whip remaining 2 cups cream with sugar to taste until quite stiff.

Loosen crust on all sides using sharp knife; remove springform. Spread all but about ½ cup cream over top of mousse. Pipe remaining cream into rosettes in center of pie.

Separate chocolate from leaves, starting at stem end of leaf. Arrange in overlapping pattern around rosettes. Cut pie into wedges with thin sharp knife.

French Silk Chocolate Pie

10 to 12 servings

½ cup (1 stick) butter, room temperature
⅔ cup sugar
2 ounces semisweet chocolate
1 teaspoon vanilla

2 eggs
1 baked 9-inch pie crust

½ cup whipping cream, whipped

Cream butter with sugar in medium bowl. Melt chocolate in top of double boiler set over hot but not boiling water. Stir in vanilla. Remove from over hot water and cool slightly. Fold into butter mixture. Add 1 egg and beat with electric mixer 5 minutes at medium speed. Add remaining egg and beat 5 more minutes. Pour mixture into pie crust. Cover tightly and refrigerate overnight.

Top slices with freshly whipped cream before serving.

Double Musky Pie

8 servings

Cracker-Pecan Crust
3 egg whites, room temperature
1/4 teaspoon cream of tartar
   Pinch of salt
1 cup sugar
30 2-inch saltine crackers, ground to
   fine crumbs
1 cup chopped pecans

Chocolate Filling
1/2 cup (1 stick) butter
2 ounces unsweetened chocolate

2 eggs
1 cup sugar
1/4 cup all purpose flour
2 teaspoons vanilla
   Vanilla ice cream

For crust: Preheat oven to 350°F. Butter 10-inch ovenproof glass deep-dish pie plate. Using electric mixer, beat whites with cream of tartar and salt in large bowl to soft peaks. Gradually add sugar and beat until stiff but not dry. Fold in cracker crumbs and pecans. Spoon into prepared pie plate, spreading up sides. Bake until lightly browned, about 12 minutes. Cool to room temperature. Press down gently against bottom and sides to form a well. Retain oven at 350°F.

For filling: Melt butter and chocolate in double boiler over gently simmering water. Stir until smooth. Cool slightly; do not allow chocolate mixture to set.

Beat eggs and sugar in medium bowl using electric mixer until slowly dissolving ribbon forms when beaters are lifted. Add flour and beat until smooth. Add chocolate mixture and vanilla and beat 1 minute. Pour into crust. Bake until set, about 35 minutes. Cool to room temperature. Serve pie with ice cream.

Grasshopper Pie

Prepared in the microwave.

6 to 8 servings

1 1/2 cups chocolate wafer crumbs
1/4 cup (1/2 stick) butter, melted

4 cups miniature marshmallows
1/2 cup milk

1/4 cup white crème de cacao
1/4 cup green crème de menthe

2 cups whipping cream, whipped
   Chocolate curls

Combine crumbs and butter in medium bowl and mix well. Press onto bottom and sides of 9-inch pie plate. Cook in microwave on High until set, about 45 seconds. Cool slightly; refrigerate.

Combine marshmallows and milk in 2-quart bowl. Cook on High until marshmallows begin to melt, about 2 to 2 1/2 minutes. Stir until completely melted. Let cool slightly. Blend in liqueurs. Let cool completely.

Fold in all but 1/2 cup whipped cream. Spoon into prepared crust. Garnish with remaining whipped cream. Sprinkle with chocolate curls. Refrigerate until firm. Serve chilled.

Pie can be prepared 1 day ahead and refrigerated.

Mocha Cream Pie

8 servings

Crust
6 tablespoons (3/4 stick) butter, melted
1½ cups chocolate wafer crumbs

Mocha Cream Filling
24 large marshmallows
½ cup milk

8 ounces semisweet chocolate
2 tablespoons crème de cacao *or* ¼ cup strong coffee
2 tablespoons coffee liqueur
1 cup whipping cream, whipped
Additional whipped cream and shaved chocolate

For crust: Combine butter and crumbs in medium bowl. Press evenly onto bottom and sides of 8-inch pie pan and set aside.

For filling: Melt marshmallows with milk in small saucepan over low heat. Let cool to room temperature. Meanwhile, melt chocolate in top of double boiler set over simmering water. Stir liqueurs into marshmallow mixture. Pour chocolate into batter and gently fold in 1 cup whipped cream. Pour into pie shell. Refrigerate until set, about 1 hour, or overnight. Garnish with additional whipped cream and shaved chocolate.

Fudge Pie

6 to 8 servings

5 ounces semisweet chocolate
¼ cup milk, heated
¼ cup dark rum
1 tablespoon instant coffee powder
1 teaspoon vanilla
Pinch of salt

1 cup whipping cream
1 baked 9-inch pie crust

Whipped cream
Chocolate curls

Melt chocolate in top of double boiler set over gently simmering wter. Stir in milk, rum, coffee powder, vanilla and salt. Remove from over water and cool to room temperature. (Do not allow mixture to set; rewarm over low heat if necessary.)

Beat cream to stiff peaks. Fold into chocolate mixture. Spoon into crust, smoothing evenly. Refrigerate 2 to 3 hours.

Before serving, cover with whipped cream and garnish with chocolate curls.

Chocolate Bavarian Hazelnut Torte

8 to 10 servings

Hazelnut Crust
1¾ cups ground toasted hazelnuts or almonds
½ cup (1 stick) unsalted butter, melted and cooled
¼ cup sugar

Chocolate Hazelnut Bavarian
6 tablespoons toasted hazelnuts or almonds
5 egg yolks, room temperature
½ cup sugar
1 cup half and half or milk
6 ounces semisweet or bittersweet chocolate, chopped

¼ cup strong coffee
¼ cup crème de cacao, rum, hazelnut, almond or coffee liqueur
1 tablespoon unflavored gelatin

1 cup whipping cream
5 egg whites, room temperature
Pinch of salt
Pinch of cream of tartar

Dark chocolate curls (garnish)

For crust: Preheat oven to 375°F. Generously butter 9-inch springform pan. Combine hazelnuts, butter and sugar in large bowl and blend well. Pat evenly into bottom and sides of pan. Bake 10 minutes. Cool completely.

For bavarian: Place nuts in processor and mix to paste. Beat egg yolks and sugar in large bowl of electric mixer at medium-high speed until thick and lemon colored. Combine half and half, chopped chocolate and nut paste in heavy large saucepan over low heat, stirring constantly until chocolate is melted. With mixer running, gradually add chocolate to yolk mixture, blending well. Transfer to saucepan and cook over medium heat, stirring constantly with wooden spoon, until mixture is thick and finger drawn across spoon leaves path; do not boil or egg yolks will curdle. Set aside.

Combine coffee and crème de cacao in small saucepan. Sprinkle gelatin over top and let stand 5 minutes. Place over medium-low heat and stir until gelatin is dissolved. Blend into chocolate.

Beat cream in medium bowl until soft peaks form (if overbeaten, bavarian will be dry and grainy). Beat egg whites in another bowl until foamy. Add salt and cream of tartar and continue beating until whites are stiff and glossy.

Set saucepan with chocolate mixture into bowl of ice water and whisk until consistency of whipped cream. Transfer to large bowl. Quickly but gently fold cream and eggs whites into chocolate mixture. Pour into prepared crust. Refrigerate until set, about 4 hours.

To serve, run sharp thin knife around crust. Remove springform. Transfer torte to serving platter and decorate top with dark chocolate curls.

Toasted Coconut Tarts

2 servings

Vanilla-Coconut Crust
- ¾ cup vanilla wafer crumbs (about 24 wafers)
- 3 tablespoons butter, melted
- 2 tablespoons grated coconut
- 5 teaspoons sugar

Coconut Filling
- ½ cup grated coconut

- 1 teaspoon unflavored gelatin
- 1½ tablespoons brandy
- 2 egg yolks, room temperature
- ¼ cup plus 2 tablespoons sugar
- ½ cup whipping cream

- 3 teaspoons apricot jam

For crust: Preheat oven to 350°F. Combine all ingredients in medium bowl. Divide mixture between two 3-inch tart pans and press evenly onto bottoms and sides. Bake until lightly browned, about 10 minutes. Let cool. Reduce oven temperature to 300°F.

For filling: Toast coconut in pie pan in oven until golden brown, stirring occasionally, 6 to 8 minutes. Set aside.

Soften gelatin in brandy in small bowl. Set bowl in larger bowl of hot water until gelatin is dissolved, shaking bowl occasionally, about 5 minutes. Beat yolks with ¼ cup sugar in medium bowl of electric mixer until very thick and pale yellow, about 3 minutes. Beat in gelatin mixture. Beat cream with remaining 2 tablespoons sugar in small bowl of electric mixer until soft peaks form. Stir cream and ¼ cup coconut into egg mixture.

Spread 1½ teaspoons jam on bottom of each crust. Mound in filling. Sprinkle remaining ¼ cup coconut over tops. Cover with plastic wrap and refrigerate until firm. Let stand at room temperature 15 minutes before serving.

Chocolate Amaretto Pie

6 to 8 servings

¼ cup (½ stick) unsalted butter
½ cup unsweetened cocoa powder
1 cup (2 sticks) unsalted butter, room temperature

1½ cups superfine sugar
¼ cup amaretto
4 eggs, room temperature
1 baked 9-inch deep-dish pie crust

Melt ¼ cup butter in heavy small saucepan. Remove from heat. Stir in cocoa powder. Cream 1 cup butter with sugar and amaretto in large bowl of electric mixer. Gradually beat in cocoa mixture. Add eggs one at a time, beating 3 minutes after each addition. Continue beating until sugar is completely dissolved. Pour into crust. Cover and refrigerate until firm, about 4 hours.

Amaretto Crème Tarts

The crisp curved wafers called tuiles *stand in for a crust in these delicate tarts.*

6 servings

Chocolate Amaretto Mousse
½ cup semisweet chocolate chips
3 tablespoons amaretto
2 tablespoons (¼ stick) unsalted butter
1 cup whipping cream

Amaretto Crème
¼ cup whipping cream

1 tablespoon sugar
1½ teaspoons amaretto
¼ teaspoon vanilla

6 tuiles (curved French cookies)

For mousse: Stir chocolate, amaretto and butter in heavy large bowl set over pan of simmering water until chocolate and butter are melted. Cool to room temperature; do not let mixture set. Beat cream in large bowl of electric mixer until stiff peaks form. Fold into chocolate mixture in batches. Chill.

For crème: Beat all ingredients in bowl of electric mixer to stiff peaks.

To assemble: Transfer mousse to pastry bag fitted with star tip. Pipe mousse into tuiles. Top each with dollop of amaretto crème and serve immediately.

Hazelnut Custard Tart

Crisp caramelized triangle torten *provide a crunchy contrast to the hazelnut custard. For best flavor, be certain that the nuts are well toasted.*

10 to 12 servings

Hazelnut Pastry
½ cup hazelnuts, toasted and husked
½ cup powdered sugar
1½ cups (3 sticks) unsalted butter, room temperature
1 egg
4 teaspoons grated orange peel
¼ teaspoon salt
2 cups pastry flour

Hazelnut Custard
2½ cups half and half, scalded
¾ cup hazelnuts, toasted and husked

½ cup sugar
1 teaspoon vanilla
Pinch of salt
¼ cup Frangelico (hazelnut liqueur)
3 eggs, room temperature
3 egg yolks, room temperature

Torten*
Powdered sugar (optional)

For pastry: Finely grind nuts with sugar in processor. Transfer to medium bowl. Add butter and beat with electric mixer until light. Mix in egg, orange peel and salt. Add flour and mix until just combined. Gather dough into ball; flatten into disc. Wrap dough in plastic and refrigerate to firm, at least 8 hours or overnight.

Dust dough with flour. Roll dough out between sheets of waxed paper to thickness of ¼ inch. Transfer to 11-inch tart pan; trim and finish edges. Refrigerate at least 30 minutes.

For custard: Combine hot half and half and hazelnuts in blender. Mix until nuts are finely chopped. Pour into heavy medium saucepan and cool.

Bring nut mixture to simmer. Strain into medium bowl. Add sugar, vanilla and salt and stir until dissolved. Mix in liqueur. Whisk eggs and yolks in another medium bowl. Slowly whisk in half and half mixture. Strain into another bowl. Cover with plastic and set aside at room temperature.

Preheat oven to 375°F. Line crust with foil, shiny side down; fill with pie weights or dried beans. Bake until set, about 20 minutes. Remove beans and foil. Continue baking until crust is light brown, 15 to 17 minutes.

Pour custard into crust. Bake until custard is just set, about 10 minutes. Let cool slightly on rack.

Just before serving, arrange *torten* upright atop custard. Dust lightly with powdered sugar.

*Torten

Makes about 14

¾ cup hazelnuts, toasted
  and husked
6 tablespoons sugar
¼ cup sliced blanched
  almonds, toasted
4 egg whites, room temperature
¼ teaspoon cream of tartar

1¼ cups (about) brown sugar, sifted
  and dried 30 minutes
  at room temperature

Preheat oven to 300°F. Butter and flour large baking sheet. Grind hazelnuts with sugar in processor. Add almonds and process until finely ground. Beat whites with cream of tartar to soft peaks in large bowl. Gently fold in nut mixture. Spread batter into ¼-inch-thick rectangle on prepared sheet. Bake until light brown, about 20 minutes. Immediately cut into 4-inch triangles. Cool on racks.

Preheat broiler. Arrange ⅓ of *torten* in single layer on baking sheet. Cover each with 2 teaspoons brown sugar. Broil 4 to 5 inches from heat until sugar melts and turns dark brown, watching carefully, about 30 seconds. Transfer to rack. Repeat with remaining *torten*. Let cool completely. Repeat on second side. Immediately transfer to rack and cool completely.

Torten can be prepared 1 day ahead. Store in airtight container.

Macadamia Chiffon Tarts

2 servings

Crust
½ cup vanilla wafer crumbs
2 tablespoons sugar
2 tablespoons (¼ stick)
  butter, melted

Filling
½ teaspoon unflavored gelatin
1 tablespoon cold water

1 egg yolk
1 tablespoon sugar
2 tablespoons boiling water

2 tablespoons dark rum
½ teaspoon grated lemon peel

1 egg white
1 tablespoon sugar
⅓ cup unsalted macadamia nuts,*
  chopped and toasted

¼ cup chilled whipping cream
1 tablespoon sugar
  Toasted chopped
  macadamia nuts

For crust: Preheat oven to 350°F. Combine all ingredients for crust in small bowl and mix well. Divide evenly between two 3-inch tart pans, pressing in gently. Bake 8 minutes. Let cool.

For filling: Sprinkle gelatin over cold water in heatproof cup and let stand 2 to 3 minutes to soften. Set cup in simmering water and stir mixture over low heat until gelatin is dissolved.

Beat egg yolk until foamy. Gradually add sugar, beating constantly until yolk is thick and lemon colored. Slowly beat in boiling water. Transfer mixture to small saucepan. Place over low heat and stir until mixture is thick enough to coat spoon. Remove from heat and stir in gelatin. Strain into bowl. Blend in rum and lemon peel. Cool custard to room temperature, stirring occasionally.

Beat egg white until foamy. Gradually add 1 tablespoon sugar and continue beating until soft peaks form. Fold into custard along with 1/3 cup macadamia nuts. Spoon into tart shells. Refrigerate until filling is set.

When ready to serve, beat cream until soft peaks form. Add remaining sugar and continue beating until stiff. Spoon onto each tart or swirl to cover completely. Sprinkle with additional toasted nuts.

*If unsalted nuts are not available, rub salted nuts vigorously in towel to remove as much salt as possible.

Chef Thomas's Pecan Cream Pie

6 to 8 servings

3/4 cup firmly packed brown sugar
1 tablespoon unflavored gelatin
1/2 teaspoon salt
1 cup sour cream
6 tablespoons (3/4 stick) butter
4 eggs, separated,
    room temperature
1 teaspoon vanilla

1 1/2 cups chopped pecans

1/2 cup sugar
1 baked 9-inch deep-dish pie crust

1 cup whipping cream
1/4 cup powdered sugar

Combine brown sugar, gelatin and salt in double boiler. Add sour cream, 3 tablespoons butter and yolks. Set over hot water and stir until mixture thickens slightly and coats back of spoon, about 8 minutes. Remove from heat. Blend in vanilla. Refrigerate until custard is thickened and mounds slightly when stirred, about 45 minutes.

Melt remaining 3 tablespoons butter in heavy small skillet. Add pecans and stir until lightly browned. Remove with slotted spoon and drain on paper towels.

Using electric mixer, beat whites to soft peaks in large bowl. Gradually add sugar and beat until stiff but not dry. Gently fold whites into custard. Mix in 1 cup pecans. Spoon into crust. Cover and refrigerate until custard is set, about 30 minutes.

Beat cream with powdered sugar to stiff peaks. Fold in remaining 1/2 cup pecans. Mound onto pie. Cut into slices and serve.

Perfect Lemon Meringue Pie

The microwave revolution-
izes preparation of this
classic dessert.

6 to 8 servings

1 frozen deep-dish 9-inch
   pie crust, unthawed
6 eggs, separated

1½ cups water
1¼ cups sugar
½ cup fresh lemon juice
⅓ cup cornstarch

¼ teaspoon salt
2 tablespoons (¼ stick) butter
2 tablespoons grated lemon peel

¼ teaspoon cream of tartar
½ cup sugar
½ teaspoon vanilla

Carefully transfer pie crust to 9-inch quiche dish or glass pie plate, fitting into pan and adjusting edge as necessary. Prick crust. Beat 1 yolk and brush over bottom and sides of pastry. Cook on High until pastry crisps and brown spots appear, about 6 to 7 minutes.

Combine next 5 ingredients in 2-quart measuring cup and stir until corn-starch is dissolved. Cook uncovered on High until thick and clear, about 7 minutes. Add butter and lemon peel and blend well. Beat remaining 5 yolks until thick. Gradually whisk into lemon mixture, blending thoroughly. Cook uncovered on High 2 minutes. Whisk again. Continue cooking uncovered on High until thickened, about 1½ minutes. Pour into partially baked shell.

Preheat oven to 300°F. Beat egg whites with cream of tartar in large bowl until foamy. Gradually add ½ cup sugar, beating constantly until glossy and soft peaks form. Beat in vanilla. Spread meringue completely over top so no filling shows. Bake until lightly browned, about 10 minutes. Let pie cool to room temperature before serving.

Tarte Citron

8 servings

Pastry
½ cup sugar
½ cup (1 stick) well-chilled butter
1½ teaspoons beaten egg
1¾ cups plus 2 tablespoons all
   purpose flour

Filling
3 eggs

1 cup sugar
6 tablespoons (¾ stick) butter,
   melted
3 tablespoons crème fraîche
½ cup fresh lemon juice
   Very finely minced peel of 3
   lemons or limes

Generously butter 10-inch tart pan with removable bottom and set aside.

For pastry: Mound sugar on work surface (preferably marble). Mix in butter with fingertips, then add egg, blending well. Stir in flour until mixture is crumbly. Knead dough until soft and pliable, about 2 to 3 minutes. Form into ball. Lightly flour work surface and roll dough into 11- to 12-inch circle ⅛ to ¼ inch thick. Fit pastry into pan. Prick bottom and sides with fork and refrigerate 1 hour.

Preheat oven to 350°F. Bake pastry until golden brown, 15 to 20 minutes.

For filling: Beat eggs lightly with sugar in medium bowl. Add butter, crème fraîche, lemon juice and peel and blend well. Ladle into crust. Bake until lightly browned, about 30 to 35 minutes. Let tart cool before serving.

Lemon Mousse Tart

A luscious dessert from one of Los Angeles's most romantic restaurants, L'Orangerie.

8 servings

Pastry
2 cups all purpose flour
¾ cup (scant) sugar
1 ounce shelled hazelnuts
  Grated peel of 1 large lime
½ cup (1 stick) plus 1 tablespoon well-chilled butter
1 egg

Lemon Mousse
3 eggs

3 egg yolks
⅔ cup fresh lemon juice
1 tablespoon grated lemon peel
¾ cup sugar
  Lemon Glaze*

Whipped cream, raspberries and mint sprigs

For pastry: Combine 1 cup flour with sugar and hazelnuts in processor and mix to fine powder. Transfer to large bowl. Stir in lime peel and remaining flour. Pound butter with rolling pin to soften slightly. Break butter into small pieces and add to flour mixture. Blend quickly with fingertips until mixture resembles coarse meal. Add egg and continue mixing until dough pulls away from sides of bowl and holds together; *do not overmix or allow butter to melt or pastry will be tough.* Divide dough in half. Gather each half into ball, then flatten into disc. Wrap in plastic. Refrigerate at least 1 hour.

Roll half of dough out on lightly floured surface to 13-inch circle (reserve remaining dough for another use). Lift dough onto rolling pin and transfer to 11-inch tart pan. Carefully press into pan, removing excess dough around edges. Prick bottom randomly with fork. Chill at least 30 minutes.

Preheat oven to 400°F. Bake pastry shell until golden brown, 10 to 12 minutes. Let cool completely.

Meanwhile, prepare mousse: Beat eggs with yolks in large bowl to blend. Add lemon juice and peel and whisk vigorously 15 seconds. Gradually add sugar, whisking constantly. Set bowl over saucepan of hot (but not boiling) water and whisk back and forth (rather than in up and down circular motion) until foamy on top and beginning to thicken, 3 to 5 minutes. Continue whisking in up and down circular motion until mixture is pale yellow and slowly dissolving ribbon forms when whisk is lifted, about 7 minutes. Immediately remove from heat and pour into cooled pastry shell. Smooth top with large spatula, spreading lemon mousse over edge of pastry. Cool tart to room temperature. Brush entire top surface with glaze. Refrigerate tart until thoroughly chilled.

To serve, top each slice with a dollop of whipped cream. Garnish with raspberries and mint.

*Lemon Glaze

Makes about 1 cup

½ cup water
6 tablespoons sugar
1 tablespoon fresh lemon juice

Combine water and sugar in small saucepan and bring to boil over medium-high heat. Let boil until syrup registers 220°F on candy thermometer. Add lemon juice and boil to 240°F (soft-ball stage). Cool about 5 minutes before using.

Fresh Lemon Tartlets

Makes about sixteen
2-inch tartlets

Pastry
1³/4 cups all purpose flour
³/4 cup (1¹/2 sticks) well-chilled
 unsalted butter, cut into
 ¹/2-inch pieces
2 tablespoons sugar
 Large pinch of salt
4 to 5 tablespoons ice water

Filling
1 cup sugar

1 lemon, cut into paper-thin slices,
 seeded and slices quartered

3 eggs, room temperature
2 tablespoons (¹/4 stick) unsalted
 butter, cut into ¹/2-inch pieces
 Candied violets

For pastry: Combine flour, butter, sugar and salt in large bowl and mix to coarse meal. Add 4 tablespoons ice water and mix just until dough can be pressed into ball, adding remaining 1 tablespoon water if necessary. Flatten into disc, wrap tightly in plastic and refrigerate for at least 1 hour.

Preheat oven to 425°F. Divide pastry in half. Return half to refrigerator. Roll remaining piece out on cool surface between 2 sheets of plastic wrap or waxed paper, loosening paper after each roll, to thickness of about ¹/8 inch. Arrange eight 2-inch (1-ounce) tartlet pans on damp towel. Drape dough over tart pans. Gently but firmly press dough into pans. Roll over tops of pans with rolling pin to cut dough to fit. Line dough with waxed paper or cupcake papers. Fill each with rice or dried beans. Bake until set, about 10 minutes. Remove beans and paper and continue baking until golden brown, about 10 more minutes. Remove pastry shells from pans and cool on rack. Repeat with remaining dough.

For filling: Combine sugar and lemon in large bowl and toss lightly until sugar is moistened. Let mixture stand for 2 hours, stirring occasionally.

Beat eggs in large bowl until thick, pale yellow and slowly dissolving ribbon forms when beaters are lifted. Stir in butter and lemon mixture. Transfer to top of double boiler. Place over simmering water and cook until thickened, stirring constantly, about 10 minutes. Let cool to room temperature. Spoon filling into prepared tart shells just before serving. Garnish with candied violets.

Lemon Tarts with Caramel

6 servings

Pâte Brisée
1 egg
1 egg yolk
3 tablespoons water

3 cups all purpose flour
¹/2 cup sugar
 Pinch of salt
1¹/4 cups (2¹/2 sticks) butter, cut
 into pieces

Caramel
¹/3 cup sugar
2 tablespoons water

Filling
3 egg yolks
1 cup sugar
2 tablespoons (¹/4 stick) unsalted
 butter, melted
 Finely grated peel and juice of
 1 lemon
2 tablespoons cornstarch
1 cup half and half

 Whipped cream
 Candied violets and
 candied mimosa

For pâte brisée: Whisk egg, yolk and water in small bowl until well blended. Combine flour, sugar and salt in medium mixing bowl. Cut in butter with pastry blender or 2 forks until mixture resembles coarse meal. Lightly blend in egg mixture. Cover with plastic wrap and refrigerate 30 minutes.

Preheat oven to 400°F. Roll pastry out to thickness of ⅛ inch. Fit into six 2- to 3-inch tart pans. Cover pastry with waxed paper and fill with dried beans. Bake until pastry is lightly browned, 18 to 20 minutes. Remove beans and paper.

For caramel: Combine sugar and water in small saucepan. Place over medium-high heat and bring to boil. Cook until mahogany colored, about 10 to 15 minutes. Pour enough caramel into each tart just to cover bottom. Let cool.

For filling: Whisk egg yolks in top of double boiler set over simmering water until thick and lemon colored. Beat in sugar and butter. Add peel and lemon juice. Combine cornstarch with a small amount of half and half in small bowl and blend until smooth. Stir in remaining half and half. Blend into yolk mixture and cook over simmering water until thick, about 30 minutes, stirring frequently. Cool. Pour filling into tart shells and refrigerate until firm.

Just before serving, spoon whipped cream into pastry bag fitted with decorative tip and pipe swirl over top of each tart. Decorate tarts with candied violets and mimosa.

Pistachio Lime Pie

8 servings

1 cup sugar
1 envelope unflavored gelatin
¼ teaspoon salt
4 eggs, separated,
   room temperature
½ cup fresh lime juice
¼ cup water
Green food coloring (optional)

1 cup whipping cream, whipped
1 baked 9-inch pie crust
⅓ cup coarsely ground
   pistachio nuts

Mix ½ cup sugar, gelatin and salt in medium saucepan. Blend yolks, lime juice and water and stir into gelatin mixture. Place over medium heat and stir just until mixture thickens and coats back of spoon, 3 to 4 minutes; *do not boil.* Transfer to bowl; stir in food coloring if desired. Refrigerate, stirring occasionally, until mixture mounds slightly on spoon, approximately 1½ hours.

Beat egg whites in large bowl of electric mixer until soft peaks form. Gradually add remaining ½ cup sugar and beat until stiff and glossy. Fold gelatin mixture into egg whites. Gently fold in whipped cream. Transfer to pie crust. Sprinkle with nuts. Refrigerate until firm.

Caribbean Lime Pie

8 to 10 servings

Coconut Pie Crust
  3 cups finely shredded
    sweetened coconut
  5 tablespoons butter, melted

Filling
½ cup fresh lime juice
1 envelope unflavored gelatin

5 egg yolks
1 cup sugar
3 tablespoons light rum

1 tablespoon orange liqueur
Grated peel of 2 limes

5 egg whites
3 drops green food coloring
   (optional)

1 cup whipping cream, whipped

1 cup whipping cream, whipped
   (optional garnish)
Lime slices

For crust: Preheat oven to 350°F. Spread thin layer of coconut over bottom of jelly roll pan and toast lightly, about 7 minutes. Reserve ½ cup for garnish.

Combine remaining coconut with melted butter in medium bowl. Toss with 2 forks until coconut is thoroughly coated with butter. Press coconut mixture firmly onto bottom and sides of deep 9-inch pie plate. Cover lightly and refrigerate until firm.

For filling: Combine lime juice and gelatin in heatproof cup and mix until gelatin is softened. Place cup in simmering water and heat until gelatin is completely liquefied, 2 to 3 minutes.

Meanwhile, combine egg yolks and ½ cup sugar in top of double boiler and beat with electric mixer to blend well. Beat in gelatin mixture. Place over simmering water and beat until mixture is thick enough to leave path when finger is drawn across spoon, about 10 minutes. Remove mixture from heat and let cool. Blend in rum, liqueur and lime peel.

Beat egg whites in large bowl of electric mixer until soft peaks form. Blend in green food coloring, if desired. With mixer at medium speed, gradually add remaining ½ cup sugar and beat until whites are stiff and glossy.

Stir 1 heaping tablespoon egg white into cooled custard, mixing well. Gently fold custard into whites with large rubber spatula, blending lightly to create marbleized effect; *do not overfold.* Gently fold in whipped cream.

Spoon filling into crust, mounding and swirling in center to create dome shape. Refrigerate or freeze until firm.

Just before serving, spoon remaining whipped cream into pastry tube fitted with star tip. Pipe rosettes over top of pie. Garnish with lime slices and sprinkle with reserved toasted coconut.

Sour Cream Lime Tarte

10 to 12 servings

Crust
1½ cups graham cracker crumbs
    (9 double crackers)
½ cup sugar
6 tablespoons (¾ stick)
    butter, melted

Filling
1 cup sugar
3 tablespoons cornstarch
1 cup whipping cream
⅓ cup fresh lime juice

¼ cup (½ stick) butter
1 tablespoon finely grated lime peel
    (2 to 3 large limes)

1 cup sour cream

Topping
1 cup whipping cream
¼ cup sugar
1½ teaspoons vanilla
¾ cup sour cream

For crust: Combine all ingredients in medium bowl. Press onto bottom and sides of 9-inch pie pan. Freeze 15 minutes.

Preheat oven to 350°F. Bake crust until lightly browned, about 12 to 15 minutes. Cool completely on rack before filling.

For filling: Mix sugar and cornstarch in heavy medium saucepan. Gradually stir in cream, lime juice, butter and lime peel. Bring to boil over medium-high heat, whisking constantly, then reduce heat to simmer and stir until thick and smooth, about 10 minutes. Cool mixture to room temperature, stirring occasionally.

Fold sour cream into cooled lime mixture. Spread evenly in prepared crust.

For topping: Whip cream with sugar and vanilla until soft peaks form. Gently fold in remaining sour cream. Spread over filling. Refrigerate for at least 4 hours before serving.

Burnt Orange Meringue Pie

This recipe comes from the Market Bar & Dining Rooms on the Concourse of New York's World Trade Center.

8 servings

1½ cups sugar
⅓ cup cornstarch
¼ teaspoon salt
1½ cups water
4 egg yolks, beaten to blend
¼ cup fresh orange juice
2 tablespoons grated orange peel

2 tablespoons (¼ stick) butter
1 baked 9-inch pie crust

4 egg whites, room temperature
¼ teaspoon cream of tartar
½ cup (8 tablespoons) sugar
2 tablespoons orange liqueur

Preheat oven to 400°F. Combine sugar, cornstarch and salt in small saucepan. Gradually add water, stirring until smooth. Place over medium heat and bring to boil, stirring constantly. Boil 1 minute, stirring constantly. Immediately pour half of hot sugar mixture into beaten egg yolks, whisking rapidly. Pour yolk mixture back into saucepan and blend thoroughly. Place over medium heat and bring to boil, stirring constantly. Boil 1 minute. Remove from heat. Stir in orange juice, grated orange peel and butter. Pour mixture into prepared pie shell.

Combine whites and cream of tartar in large bowl of electric mixer and beat until soft peaks form. Gradually beat in sugar 2 tablespoons at a time, beating well after each addition. Continue beating until whites are stiff but not dry. Fold in orange liqueur.

Spread meringue over pie filling, sealing carefully to edges of crust. Bake until meringue is just golden, about 9 minutes. Cool on rack at least 1 hour before slicing and serving.

Orange Tart

From André Soltner, the chef at New York's renowned restaurant Lutèce.

8 servings

Crust
1¼ cups all purpose flour
1 tablespoon sugar
½ cup (1 stick) well-chilled butter
3 tablespoons (about) ice water

Orange Filling
1 envelope unflavored gelatin
3 tablespoons cold water
1 cup milk

4 egg yolks, room temperature
¾ cup sugar
2 tablespoons Grand Marnier

1 cup well-chilled whipping cream

3 oranges
3 tablespoons Grand Marnier
1 tablespoon sugar

For crust: Combine flour and sugar in large bowl. Cut in butter until pea-size pieces form. Using fork, mix in enough water to just bind dough; do not knead. Form into ball and flatten into disc. Wrap in plastic; chill at least 1 hour.

Preheat oven to 400°F. Roll dough out on lightly floured surface to 13-inch round. Transfer to 10-inch tart pan with removable bottom. Fold in overhanging dough, forming double edge. Pinch decoratively. Line crust with parchment and fill with pie weights or dried beans. Bake 20 minutes. Remove pie weights and paper and bake until crust is golden brown, 8 to 10 minutes longer. Cool.

For filling: Soften gelatin in 3 tablespoons water in small bowl. Scald milk in heavy medium saucepan. Mix yolks with sugar in medium bowl. Slowly whisk in hot milk. Return mixture to saucepan. Stir over medium-low heat until mixture leaves path on back of spoon when finger is drawn across or registers 175°F on thermometer; do not boil. Add gelatin and stir until dissolved. Strain custard through fine sieve into chilled metal bowl. Mix in 2 tablespoons Grand Marnier. Refrigerate until completely cool and beginning to thicken, stirring frequently.

Whip cream until just beginning to mound softly. Fold into custard. Pour into cooled crust. Refrigerate until set, at least 2 hours. (*Can be prepared 1 day ahead; cover tightly with plastic.*)

Remove peel from oranges (colored part only) using vegetable peeler. Cut into very fine julienne. Mix with 3 tablespoons Grand Marnier and 1 tablespoon sugar. Let stand 1 hour.

Cut all white pith from oranges. Slice oranges thinly. Drain on paper towels. Just before serving, drain orange peel. Top tart with orange slices and peel.

Pumpkin Chiffon Pie

A total food processor preparation—crust, filling and topping. To guarantee that cream will whip, place 2 tablespoons nonfat dry milk powder into work bowl, then pour cream through feed tube with machine running.

8 servings

Crust
6 ounces gingersnap cookies (about 24)
5 tablespoons unsalted butter, melted
3 tablespoons firmly packed light brown sugar
½ teaspoon cinnamon

Filling
2 tablespoons water
2 tablespoons dark rum
2 teaspoons unflavored gelatin

¾ cup sugar
3 egg yolks
1½ cups solid pack canned pumpkin (12 ounces)

½ cup milk
½ teaspoon cinnamon
½ teaspoon freshly grated nutmeg
Pinch of salt

1 tablespoon fresh lemon juice
1 tablespoon water
4 egg whites

Topping
2 tablespoons nonfat dry milk powder (optional)
1 cup well-chilled whipping cream
2 tablespoons powdered sugar
1 tablespoon dark rum

For crust: Position rack in center of oven and preheat to 350°F. Butter 6-cup deep-dish glass or metal pie plate (do not use ceramic dish).

Chop gingersnaps in processor using 4 on/off turns, then process to uniform fine crumbs. Add melted butter, brown sugar and cinnamon and blend 10 seconds. Press crumb mixture firmly into bottom and sides of prepared pie plate (use bottom of drinking glass to help press crumbs into bottom edge). Bake 6 minutes. (If crust slips during baking, reshape with hands while still hot.) Let cool completely. (*Crust can be prepared up to 1 month ahead and frozen. Thaw before proceeding.*)

For filling: Combine water and rum in cup. Sprinkle gelatin over top. Let stand until softened, about 5 minutes.

Combine sugar and yolks in processor and blend 1 minute, stopping once to scrape down sides of work bowl. Add pumpkin, milk, spices and salt and mix 10 seconds. Transfer to top of double boiler set over gently simmering water. Cook, stirring constantly, until filling is slightly thickened, about 10 minutes; *do not boil or yolks will curdle.* Blend in gelatin mixture. Refrigerate filling until thickened but not set.

Combine lemon juice and water in cup. Clean work bowl and blade; reinsert steel knife. Whip egg whites in work bowl 8 seconds. With machine running, pour lemon juice mixture through feed tube and process until whites hold shape, about 1½ minutes. Gently spoon pumpkin mixture evenly over whites and blend using 2 on/off turns. Run spatula around inside of work bowl. Blend using 2 more on/off turns (some streaks of egg white will remain; do not overprocess).

Using rubber spatula, turn filling into cooled crust, mounding slightly in center. Refrigerate pie at least 2 hours. (*Can be prepared up to 1 day ahead.*)

Just before serving, prepare topping: Place milk powder in work bowl if using. With machine running, pour cream through feed tube and whip until thickened, about 1 minute; do not overprocess. Add powdered sugar and rum and blend 5 seconds. Spoon cream into pastry bag fitted with medium star tip. Pipe rosettes of cream decoratively over top of pie.

Sherry-Pumpkin Chiffon Pie

8 servings

3 eggs, separated
½ cup sugar
1 cup canned pumpkin
½ cup half and half
1 teaspoon cinnamon
½ teaspoon freshly grated nutmeg
½ teaspoon salt
⅛ teaspoon ground ginger

1 tablespoon unflavored gelatin
½ cup sweet Sherry
2 tablespoons (¼ stick) butter, room temperature
1 teaspoon vanilla

1 baked 9-inch pie crust
Whipped cream

Beat yolks with sugar in medium bowl of electric mixer. Add pumpkin, half and half, cinnamon, nutmeg, salt and ginger and mix well. Transfer to medium saucepan and stir over low heat until mixture thickens, 4 to 5 minutes. Soften gelatin in Sherry. Stir into pumpkin mixture. Blend in butter and vanilla. Transfer filling to bowl. Cover and refrigerate until thickened but not set, about 1 hour.

Beat egg whites until stiff but not dry. Fold into filling. Spoon into pie crust. Refrigerate until firm. Decorate pie with whipped cream and serve chilled.

Sour Cream Pumpkin Pie

This is best served the day it is baked.

6 servings

¼ cup sugar
1 teaspoon cinnamon
½ teaspoon ground ginger
¼ teaspoon freshly grated nutmeg
¼ teaspoon salt
⅛ teaspoon ground cloves
1½ cups pumpkin puree
3 egg yolks, room temperature
1 cup sour cream

3 egg whites, room temperature
Pinch of cream of tartar
½ cup sugar
1 partially baked 9-inch pie crust
Whipped cream (optional)

Preheat oven to 350°F. Mix ¼ cup sugar, cinnamon, ginger, nutmeg, salt and cloves in top of double boiler. Blend in pumpkin puree, yolks and sour cream. Stir over simmering water until thick, about 15 minutes.

Beat whites with cream of tartar until soft peaks form. Gradually beat in ½ cup sugar until whites are stiff but not dry. Fold into pumpkin mixture. Turn into pie shell. Bake until top is brown, about 45 minutes. Cool pie completely. Top with whipped cream if desired.

Pumpkin Pie with Candied Orange Peel

8 servings

Pastry
1 cup unbleached all purpose flour
1 tablespoon sugar
Pinch of salt
8 tablespoons (1 stick) well-chilled unsalted butter, cut into ½-inch pieces
2 tablespoons ice water (or more)

1 egg beaten with
1 tablespoon water

Pumpkin-Ginger Filling
1 cup lightly packed light brown sugar
1 teaspoon cinnamon
¾ to 1 teaspoon ground ginger
½ teaspoon freshly grated nutmeg

¼ teaspoon salt
1½ cups pureed cooked pumpkin
1 tablespoon molasses
1 cup whipping cream
2 eggs, lightly beaten to blend
¼ cup orange marmalade
2 tablespoons Grand Marnier

Candied Orange Peel
2 large oranges
2 cups water
½ cup sugar
¼ cup water
1 tablespoon Grand Marnier plus 3 tablespoons water *or* ¼ cup fresh orange juice

1 cup whipping cream
2 tablespoons powdered sugar

For pastry: Sift flour, sugar and salt into large bowl. Cut in butter until mixture resembles coarse meal. Sprinkle with 2 tablespoons ice water and stir quickly with fork until dough just holds together, adding 1 to 2 teaspoons more water if necessary. Turn dough out onto waxed paper. Pat into 5- to 6-inch disc. Sprinkle lightly with flour. Wrap tightly in waxed paper. Refrigerate at least 2 hours. (*Dough can be prepared 2 to 3 days ahead and refrigerated or frozen.*)

Butter 9-inch metal pie pan or glass pie plate. Roll dough out on lightly floured surface into 10-inch circle. Gently fit dough into prepared pan. Fold overlap back under, forming double thickness on rim; crimp edges decoratively. Prick bottom with fork at ¼-inch intervals. Refrigerate pastry shell for 1 hour.

Preheat oven to 425°F (400°F for glass). Line pastry shell with aluminum foil. Fill with rice, dried beans or pie weights. Bake until set, about 7 to 8 minutes. Remove rice and foil from shell. Brush pastry with egg mixture. Bake until golden brown, 15 to 20 minutes.

For filling: Position rack in center of oven and preheat to 350°F. Blend sugar, cinnamon, ginger, nutmeg and salt in large bowl. Whisk in pumpkin and molasses, then add cream and eggs. Stir in marmalade and liqueur. Pour filling into partially baked pastry. Bake until filling is almost set, about 55 to 60 minutes. Let pie cool on wire rack for at least 2 hours.

For orange peel: Remove peel from oranges in 2-inch-wide strips using vegetable peeler. Slice lengthwise into very thin julienne. Bring 2 cups water to rapid boil in heavy saucepan. Add orange peel and blanch 5 minutes. Drain well. Add sugar and ¼ cup water to saucepan. Cook over low heat until sugar is dissolved, swirling pan occasionally. Return peel to saucepan. Place over medium heat and boil until most of liquid is evaporated and mixture is pale golden brown, swirling pan occasionally, about 5 minutes. Remove from heat. Gradually stir in liqueur mixture. Cool to room temperature; if orange peel crystallizes, add 2 more tablespoons liquid and heat gently until sugar dissolves.

Just before serving, whip cream to very soft peaks. Add sugar and continue whipping until stiff enough to hold shape on spoon. Mound about ¾ cup cream in center of pie. Sprinkle with orange peel. Pass remaining cream separately.

🍒 Cheese Pies

Cream Cheese Pie with Sour Cream Topping

A microwave filling using an unusual cook-and-stir technique.

8 servings

1 pound cream cheese,
   room temperature
2 eggs
½ cup sugar
1 tablespoon grated lemon peel
1½ teaspoons vanilla

Pinch of salt
1 cup sour cream
1 9-inch graham cracker crust

1 cup sour cream
¼ cup sugar

Combine cream cheese and eggs in small bowl and beat until fluffy. Add sugar, lemon peel, vanilla and salt and blend well. Mix in 1 cup sour cream. Cook on High 8 minutes, stopping every 2 minutes to mix with whisk. Pour into crust and let cool.

    Combine remaining sour cream and sugar and blend well. Spread over pie. Chill thoroughly before serving.

Lemon Cheese Pie

6 to 8 servings

3 eggs
½ cup sugar
8 ounces cream cheese,
   room temperature
½ cup cottage cheese
1 9-inch graham cracker crust

1 14-ounce can sweetened
   condensed milk
⅓ cup fresh lemon juice
   Grated lemon peel

Preheat oven to 350°F. Using electric mixer, beat eggs until thick, 2 to 3 minutes. Gradually beat in sugar. Add cheeses and blend until smooth. Pour into crust. Bake 35 minutes. Cool pie 15 minutes.

    Combine condensed milk and lemon juice. Spread over top of pie. Cover and refrigerate overnight. Garnish pie with grated peel.

Cherry Cream Cheese Pie

8 servings

8 ounces cream cheese, room
   temperature
½ cup sifted powdered sugar
½ teaspoon vanilla

1 cup whipping cream, whipped
1 baked 9-inch deep-dish pie crust
1 21-ounce can cherry pie filling,
   well chilled

Whip cream cheese with sugar until fluffy. Blend in vanilla. Fold in whipped cream, blending thoroughly. Spoon into pie shell. Spread cherries evenly over top. Refrigerate pie several hours or overnight.

🍒

Cheesecake Tart and Wine-glazed Fruit

10 to 12 servings

Almond Crust
1½ cups all purpose flour
 1 cup sliced almonds, finely ground
   (do not use blanched almonds)
 ½ cup (1 stick) unsalted butter,
   room temperature
 ¼ cup sugar
 1 egg, beaten to blend
 1 teaspoon vanilla

Cream Cheese Filling
 2 eggs, separated

 ½ cup sugar
 1 pound cream cheese,
   room temperature
 1 tablespoon fresh lemon juice
 1 teaspoon grated lemon peel
 ½ teaspoon vanilla
   Pinch of cream of tartar

 3 kiwis, peeled and sliced
 1 pint strawberries
   Rosé Wine Glaze*

For crust: Mix all ingredients using heavy-duty mixer or by hand. Press dough evenly into 11-inch tart pan. Trim and finish edges. Pierce all over with fork. Refrigerate 30 minutes.

Preheat oven to 375°F. Line crust with parchment or foil and fill with pie weights or dried beans. Bake until dough is set, about 20 minutes. Remove weights and paper. Pierce crust again. Bake until golden brown, about 10 minutes. Cool 5 minutes. Reduce oven temperature to 350°F.

For filling: Using electric mixer, beat yolks and sugar until pale. Add cream cheese, lemon juice, lemon peel and vanilla. Beat until smooth. Beat whites and cream of tartar in another bowl until stiff but not dry. Fold ¼ of whites into cheese mixture to lighten; fold in remaining whites. Spoon into crust. Bake until filling is firm to touch, about 20 minutes. Cool completely on rack. Refrigerate at least 1 hour. (*Can be prepared 1 day ahead.*)

Overlap kiwi slices in center of tart. Place 1 strawberry on top. Thinly slice remaining berries. Arrange in overlapping rows around kiwis to edge of tart. Spoon glaze over fruit. Refrigerate at least 15 minutes. (*Can be prepared 2 hours ahead.*) Let stand at room temperature 20 minutes before serving.

Rosé Wine Glaze

Makes about ¾ cup

 ¾ cup apple jelly
 1 tablespoon rosé
 1 teaspoon sugar

Heat all ingredients in heavy small saucepan over low heat, swirling pan occasionally, until jelly melts and sugar dissolves. Increase heat and boil until syrupy, about 6 minutes.

Chocolate Mousse Pie with Raspberry Sauce

6 to 8 servings

 4 ounces semisweet chocolate
 2 tablespoons milk

 8 ounces cream cheese,
   room temperature
 3 tablespoons sugar
 ⅓ cup Grand Marnier
1¾ cups whipping cream, whipped
 1 9-inch graham cracker crust

 2 10-ounce packages frozen
   raspberries, thawed and drained
 ¼ cup Grand Marnier

 1 cup whipping cream, whipped
 2 ounces semisweet chocolate,
   grated

Combine 4 ounces chocolate and milk in small saucepan over very low heat. Stir until chocolate melts, 1 to 2 minutes. Cool.

Beat cream cheese and sugar until smooth and well mixed, 2 to 3 minutes. Add ⅓ cup Grand Marnier and cooled chocolate mixture and blend well. Gently fold in whipped cream. Spoon into crust. Cover and refrigerate at least 2 hours or overnight.

Combine raspberries and Grand Marnier in food processor and puree. Strain into small bowl to eliminate seeds. Chill at least 2 hours or overnight.

Just before serving, pipe rosettes of whipped cream around outside edge of pie. Sprinkle with grated chocolate. Pass sauce separately.

Strawberry Tartlets with Mascarpone Buttercream

For the best texture and flavor, use very fresh mascarpone cheese.

Makes 8

Pâte Brisée (see page 2)

Buttercream Filling
1½ cups mascarpone cheese*
   (about 12 ounces)
 3 tablespoons sugar
⅔ cup well-chilled whipping cream

6 cups small strawberries, hulled
⅓ cup red currant-raspberry jelly or red currant jelly, melted

Cut pâte brisée into 8 pieces and form into rounds. Place 7 pieces in refrigerator. Roll out remaining piece between sheets of plastic wrap or waxed paper to 5-inch round. (If dough is too soft to handle, refrigerate or freeze 5 minutes to firm.) Arrange in 4-inch tart pan. Trim and finish edges. Repeat with remaining pastry. Cover tartlets and refrigerate 30 minutes.

Preheat oven to 425°F. Pierce pastry all over with fork. Line with foil and fill with pie weights or dried beans. Bake 10 minutes. Remove foil and weights and continue baking until crusts are pale golden brown, about 7 minutes. Cool 5 minutes on rack. Remove from pans and cool on rack.

For filling: Mix mascarpone and sugar with fork until blended. Mix in cream 1 tablespoon at a time.

Spread 3 tablespoons filling over each crust. Arrange berries on top, stem side down. Brush berries with jelly. Spoon remaining filling into pastry bag fitted with small star tip. Pipe decoratively around edge of tarts.

Tarts can be prepared 1 hour ahead.

*Available at Italian markets.

Sifnos Honey Pie

This Greek specialty has a sweet cheese filling in a tender crust.

8 servings

Crust
 2 cups cake flour
 2 tablespoons sugar
½ teaspoon baking powder
   Pinch of salt
½ cup (1 stick) unsalted butter, room temperature
 1 tablespoon (about) cold water

Honey Cheese Filling
 1 pound fresh mezíthra cheese,*
   crumbled, or ricotta cheese

½ cup sugar
 1 teaspoon cinnamon
¾ cup honey
 4 eggs, beaten to blend
 1 tablespoon grated lemon peel

   Cinnamon

For crust: Butter 10-inch pie pan. Sift flour, sugar, baking powder and salt into medium bowl. Cut in butter until coarse meal forms. Knead, adding enough water to form stiff dough. (If dough is too soft to handle, wrap in plastic and refrigerate 20 minutes to firm.) Pat dough into prepared pan. Flute edges decoratively.

For filling: Using electric mixer, beat cheese, sugar and 1 teaspoon cinnamon in large bowl until well combined. Mix in honey, eggs and peel.

Position rack in center of oven and preheat to 350°F. Pour filling into dough-lined pan. Bake pie until firm, about 50 minutes, covering crust with foil if browning too quickly. Cool completely on rack. Sprinkle pie with cinnamon before serving.

*Available at Greek and Middle Eastern markets and some specialty food stores.

Peanut Butter Cream Cheese Pie

6 to 8 servings

Pecan Crust
- 1½ cups pecans, toasted and finely chopped
- ½ cup sugar
- ¼ cup clarified butter
- ¼ teaspoon cinnamon

Filling
- 1 cup whipping cream

- 1¼ cups powdered sugar
- 1 tablespoon vanilla
- 8 ounces cream cheese, room temperature
- 1 cup creamy peanut butter
- 2 tablespoons clarified butter

- ½ cup chocolate fudge topping

For crust: Mix all ingredients in 9-inch metal pie pan; press into bottom and sides. Freeze crust until ready to use.

For filling: Using electric mixer, beat cream with ¼ cup powdered sugar and vanilla to stiff peaks in large bowl. Beat remaining 1 cup powdered sugar, cream cheese, peanut butter and clarified butter in another large bowl until fluffy. Fold in half of whipped cream. (Refrigerate remaining cream.) Spoon into crust. Cover and refrigerate until firm, about 2 hours.

Spread fudge topping over pie, leaving 1-inch border. Rebeat reserved cream briefly if necessary and spoon around border. Refrigerate pie for at least 1 hour before serving.

Peanut Butter Mint Pie

6 to 8 servings

- 3 ounces cream cheese, room temperature
- ¾ cup sugar
- ½ cup milk, room temperature
- ⅓ cup creamy peanut butter

- 1 cup whipping cream, whipped
- 1 4-ounce mint chocolate bar, finely chopped
- 1 9-inch graham cracker crust
- Whipped cream (garnish)

Combine cream cheese, sugar, milk and peanut butter in large bowl of electric mixer and beat well. Fold in whipped cream and mint chocolate. Pour mixture into crust. Refrigerate overnight. Garnish with whipped cream.

Pecan-Cream Cheese Pie

8 servings

1 unbaked 9-inch pie crust

1 pound cream cheese, room temperature
¼ cup sugar
1 egg
2 teaspoons vanilla

3 eggs
¾ cup light corn syrup
1 teaspoon vanilla

3 ounces pecans, lightly toasted and finely chopped

Preheat oven to 375°F. Line pie crust with waxed paper, fill with dried beans, rice or pie weights and bake for 10 minutes. Remove paper and weights; retain oven temperature.

Combine cream cheese, ¼ cup sugar, 1 egg and 2 teaspoons vanilla in large bowl and beat until smooth.

In another bowl beat eggs, corn syrup and remaining sugar and vanilla until well mixed.

Pour cream cheese mixture into pie crust, spreading evenly. Sprinkle with pecans. Stir corn syrup mixture again and carefully pour through fork over pecans (*this technique will keep pecans from shifting*). Bake until set, about 40 to 45 minutes. Let pie cool, then refrigerate. Serve chilled.

Ginger-Pumpkin Pie

Made in the microwave.

8 to 12 servings

Crust
⅓ cup butter or margarine
1¼ cups gingersnap cookie crumbs (about 20 cookies)

Filling
8 ounces cream cheese
1 cup canned pumpkin
¾ cup firmly packed brown sugar

3 eggs, beaten
1½ tablespoons all purpose flour
1 teaspoon ground ginger
1 teaspoon cinnamon
¼ teaspoon ground allspice or cloves
Candied ginger and chopped nuts

For crust: Melt butter on High in 9-inch microwave-safe pie plate, about 1 minute. Stir in crumbs; press firmly into bottom and sides of plate. Cook on High 1 to 1½ minutes. Set crust aside to cool.

For filling: Place cream cheese in medium-size glass bowl and soften on Medium (50 percent power), about 1½ to 2 minutes. Beat until smooth. Add pumpkin, sugar, eggs, flour, ginger, cinnamon and allspice or cloves and continue beating until smooth. Cook filling on Medium (50 percent power) until thickened, about 7 to 9 minutes, stirring frequently. Pour filling into crust. Cook on Medium (50 percent power) until firm, about 10 minutes. Let cool (pie will continue to set as it cools). Refrigerate until ready to serve. Garnish with candied ginger and chopped nuts.

4 ❦ Nut and Chess Pies

At the mention of nut pies, chances are you think of the classic pecan version. To be sure, pecan pie is the most familiar of all, and we've selected several pleasing variations—among them simple Blue Ribbon Pecan Pie (page 92), rich Butter-Rum Pecan Tart (page 93), and Chocolate Pecan Pie (page 95).

But don't limit yourself to pecans, because other types of nuts have wonderful flavors of their own. Deux Cheminées Walnut Tart (page 97) boasts an opulently sweet filling that resembles caramel. The buttery crust and rich filling of Coconut-Almond Tart (page 90) make it the perfect finale to an epicurean dinner. For a dessert a bit on the unusual side, consider Marshall Islands Macadamia Nut Pie (page 91) or crunchy Pine Nut Tart (page 91). And if you just can't decide on one flavor, the Six-Nut Tart on page 100 will solve your dilemma.

Chess pies are a Southern specialty, with an emphasis on *special*. It is amazing how anything so luxuriously rich—there's no stinting on eggs, sugar or butter—can be so easy to prepare. Ten minutes is all it takes to stir up a chess pie, even less if you use a food processor. Chocolate Chess Pie (page 106) is one of the most popular types. But don't overlook our other tempting recipes; for example, Aunt Catfish's Boatsinker (page 107), though amusingly named, is a dream come true for the most serious of chocolate lovers.

Almond Pie

16 servings

2½ cups graham cracker crumbs
½ cup (1 stick) butter,
　room temperature
½ cup milk
　Graham cracker crumbs

1¾ cups whipping cream
1 14-ounce can sweetened
　condensed milk

2 eggs
½ cup dark raisins
½ cup chopped blanched almonds

Butter 12-inch flan or tart pan. Combine 2½ cups crumbs with ½ cup butter in processor or mixing bowl and blend to paste. Add milk, mixing until smooth dough is formed. Dust work surface with graham cracker crumbs. Working quickly, roll out dough and fit into pan, patting gently into sides. Set aside in freezer while preparing filling.

Preheat oven to 300°F. Combine remaining ingredients in medium bowl and beat until well blended. Pour into pie shell. Bake until filling is light golden and center is set, about 50 minutes. Cool pie on rack before serving.

Lemon and Almond Pie

6 to 8 servings

Pastry
1⅓ cups plus 1 tablespoon
　sifted flour
⅓ cup sugar
¼ teaspoon salt
⅓ cup well-chilled unsalted butter,
　cut into small pieces
3 egg yolks
½ teaspoon vanilla

Filling
3 eggs
¾ cup sugar
7 tablespoons fresh lemon juice
1 heaping tablespoon finely grated
　lemon peel
1 cup ground blanched almonds
⅔ cup unsalted butter, melted

For pastry: Combine flour, sugar and salt in large bowl and blend well. Cut in butter with pastry blender until mixture resembles coarse meal. Beat yolks with vanilla. Add to flour mixture and blend until dough holds together. Press dough into ball; flatten into disc. Wrap in plastic and refrigerate 1 hour or longer.

Position rack in lower third of oven and preheat to 375°F. Roll dough out on lightly floured board to thickness of about ⅛ inch. Fit into 10-inch pie plate or flan ring; trim excess dough 1 inch beyond rim of pan. Flute edges. Line crust with waxed or parchment paper. Set slightly smaller pan or pie plate inside crust and fill with dried beans or pie weights. Bake 10 to 12 minutes. Let cool slightly before removing inside pan, then let pastry stand until completely cooled.

For filling: Beat eggs and sugar together until light and lemon colored. Stir in lemon juice and peel. Add almonds and butter. Pour into pastry and bake until filling is golden brown and set, 25 to 30 minutes. Serve at room temperature.

Pie can be baked 6 to 8 hours ahead, but is best baked and served on the same day.

Swiss Chocolate Almond Pie

8 servings

Crust
- 2 cups all purpose flour
- ³/₄ cup (1¹/₂ sticks) unsalted butter, cut into small pieces
- ³/₄ cup sliced almonds, coarsely chopped
- ¹/₄ cup firmly packed brown sugar
- 1 ounce semisweet chocolate (preferably Swiss), grated
- ¹/₄ teaspoon salt
- 1 tablespoon Swiss chocolate almond cordial
- ¹/₂ teaspoon almond extract
  Water

Filling
- ¹/₂ cup (1 stick) butter, room temperature
- ²/₃ cup sugar
- 2 ounces unsweetened chocolate, melted and cooled
- 2 eggs
- 1 tablespoon Swiss chocolate almond cordial
- ¹/₂ teaspoon almond extract

Topping
- 2 cups whipping cream
- ¹/₄ cup powdered sugar
- 2 tablespoons Swiss chocolate almond cordial

For crust: Preheat oven to 375°F. Generously grease 9-inch pie plate. Combine flour and butter in medium bowl and mix with fingertips until consistency of coarse meal. Gently blend in almonds, sugar, chocolate and salt. Remove ¹/₂ cup mixture for garnish. Sprinkle cordial and almond extract over remaining mixture and toss together, adding water as needed, until dough can be formed into ball.

Press into bottom and sides of prepared pie plate. Bake until crust is set and almonds are browned, about 15 minutes. Spread reserved mixture on baking sheet and bake until browned, about 5 minutes. Let cool. Chop and reserve crumb mixture for garnish.

For filling: Cream butter in medium bowl. Gradually add sugar and beat until mixture is light and fluffy. Stir in chocolate. Add eggs one at a time, beating well after each addition. Stir in cordial and almond extract. Turn into prepared crust, spreading evenly. Chill.

For topping: Shortly before serving, beat all topping ingredients in large bowl until stiff. Spoon into pastry bag fitted with large star tip and pipe over filling. Garnish pie with reserved crumbs.

Hazelnut-Orange Pithiviers

A traditional French pastry, a Pithiviers *consists of a sweet nut filling encased in a rich puff pastry shell.*

12 servings

Pastry
- 4 cups all purpose flour
- 1 teaspoon salt
- 2³/₄ cups (5¹/₂ sticks) well-chilled unsalted butter, cut into ¹/₂-inch cubes
- 1 cup (about) cold water

Hazelnut-Orange Filling
- 5 ounces hazelnuts, toasted and partially husked
- ¹/₂ cup sugar
- 4 teaspoons grated orange peel
- 3 tablespoons unsalted butter, room temperature
- 2¹/₂ tablespoons orange liqueur
- 1 egg
- 1 egg yolk
- 2 drops almond extract
  Pinch of salt

- 1 egg yolk beaten with 1 tablespoon water (glaze)

  Powdered sugar

For pastry: Sift flour and salt into large bowl. Using pastry blender or 2 kinves, cut in butter to ¼-inch pieces. Stir in enough water so dough just comes together. (Dough will look lumpy and unblended.)

Roll dough out on lightly floured surface into 12 × 16-inch rectangle. Using pastry scraper, fold dough into 3 equal sections as for business letter. Give dough quarter turn so it opens like a book. (This is a single turn.) Roll, fold and turn dough 3 more times for total of 4 single turns. Wrap dough in plastic. Chill at least 2 hours or overnight.

For filling: Mix hazelnuts, sugar and peel to powder in processor. Add butter, liqueur, egg, yolk, almond extract and salt and blend until smooth. Cover and chill until ready to use.

To assemble: Divide dough into thirds. (Wrap 2 pieces and refrigerate or freeze for another use.) Cut remaining piece into 2 pieces, 1 slightly larger than the other. Roll smaller piece out on lightly floured surface to thickness of ¹⁄₁₆ inch. Cut out 10-inch circle. Roll remaining dough out on lightly floured surface to thickness of ⅛ inch. Cut out 11-inch circle. Gather scraps and set aside. Set 10-inch circle on baking sheet. Shape filling into 4-inch mound in center of dough. Brush edges with water. Top with 11-inch circle, pressing around filling to eliminate air and pressing edges together to seal. Make incision in top of dough to allow steam to escape. Roll out scraps. Cut out decorations. Affix around incision. Using sharp paring knife, score curved lines from center to edge of pastry without cutting through. Cut edges in scallop pattern. Brush tart with some of glaze; do not allow to drip over edges. Refrigerate at least 15 minutes.

Preheat oven to 450°F. Brush tart with remaining glaze. Set in oven. Reduce oven temperature to 400°F. Bake 15 minutes. Reduce oven temperature to 350°F. Bake until golden brown, 20 to 25 minutes. Remove from oven.

Position rack in top of oven and increase temperature to 450°F. Sprinkle tart generously with powdered sugar. Bake until sugar caramelizes slightly, watching carefully, 3 to 4 minutes. Cool briefly on rack. Serve Pithiviers warm or at room temperature.

Pecan Fudge Tarts

2 servings

Crust
- ¾ cup all purpose flour
- ½ teaspoon sugar
- Pinch of salt
- 3 tablespoons butter, cut into pieces
- 2 tablespoons (about) ice water

Filling
- 2 tablespoons (¼ stick) butter
- 1½ tablespoons unsweetened cocoa powder
- ¼ cup hot water
- 2 tablespoons milk
- ½ cup sugar
- 2 tablespoons all purpose flour
- ¼ teaspoon vanilla
- Pinch of salt
- ¼ cup coarsely chopped pecans

For crust: Combine flour, sugar and salt in bowl. Cut in butter using pastry blender or 2 knives until mixture resembles coarse meal. Using fork, stir in enough water so dough just comes together; do not overwork. Gather into ball. Wrap in plastic; chill 15 minutes.

Press dough into bottom and sides of two 4½-inch tart pans with removable bottoms. Chill until ready to bake.

For filling: Preheat oven to 375°F. Melt butter in heavy small saucepan. Remove from heat. Stir in cocoa powder until smooth. Blend in water and milk. Whisk in sugar, flour, vanilla and salt. Stir in pecans. Pour into tart shells. Bake until filling is firm, 30 minutes. Serve at room temperature.

Bountiful Hot Fudge Sundae Pie

Hazelnut Custard Tart

Brian Leatart

Brian Leatart

Coffee Chiffon Pie

Peppered Apple-Cheese Tart

Top: Walnut Lace Tart
Bottom: Pumpkin Pie with Candied Orange Peel

Brian Leatart

Tomato-Orange Tart

Country Apple Tart

Pecan Tassies

Makes 24

Cream Cheese Pastry
- ½ cup (1 stick) unsalted butter, room temperature
- 3 ounces cream cheese, room temperature
- 1 cup unbleached all purpose flour

Pecan Filling
- ¾ cup firmly packed light brown sugar
- 1 egg
- 2 tablespoons (¼ stick) unsalted butter, room temperature
- 2 tablespoons sour mash bourbon
- 1 teaspoon vanilla
- Pinch of salt
- 1 cup coarsely chopped pecans, toasted

For pastry: Using electric mixer, cream butter and cream cheese. Add flour and beat just until dough comes together; do not overmix. Wrap in plastic. Chill until firm, at least 2 hours.

For filling: Blend sugar, egg, butter, bourbon, vanilla and salt.

To assemble: Preheat oven to 350°F. Lightly butter 24 miniature tartlet pans or muffin cups. Roll dough out on lightly floured surface to thickness of ⅛ inch. Cut out 24 rounds, using 2¼-inch cutter. Reroll scraps as necessary. Fit rounds into prepared pans or cups; trim edges. Divide pecans among tartlets. Pour in filling. Bake until filling has set and cracked slightly, 25 to 30 minutes. Cool in pans on rack.

Walnut Tart (Tarte aux Noix)

A buttery crust contrasts with rich custardlike filling in this superb pastry from the Hotel Cro-Magnon in Les Eyzies, France.

6 to 8 servings

Pastry
- 1½ cups plus 3 tablespoons all purpose flour
- 6 tablespoons powdered sugar
- 7 tablespoons well-chilled unsalted butter, cut into small pieces
- 2 egg yolks
- 1 teaspoon vanilla

Filling
- 1 cup plus 1½ tablespoons whipping cream
- 1 cup powdered sugar
- ¾ cup walnut powder (from about 3½ ounces walnuts)
- 2 egg yolks
- 1 teaspoon vanilla
- Pinch of cinnamon

- Walnut halves

For pastry: Combine flour and sugar in large bowl. Cut in butter until mixture resembles coarse meal. Blend in yolks and vanilla. Gather dough into ball. Turn out onto lightly floured surface. Using heel of hand, smear dough a little at a time across surface to blend butter and flour thoroughly. Flatten into disc. Wrap and refrigerate 1 hour.

Preheat oven to 400°F. Roll dough out between sheets of waxed paper to thickness of ⅛ inch. Fit into 11-inch tart pan with removable bottom; trim edges. Pierce shell with fork. Line with parchment or foil; fill with dried beans or pie weights. Bake until pastry is set, about 10 minutes. Reduce oven temperature to 350°F. Remove beans and foil. Bake until crust is golden brown, approximately 10 minutes.

For filling: Reduce oven temperature to 300°F. Blend all ingredients. Pour into crust. Bake until filling is set and looks dry, about 35 minutes. Cool completely. Decorate with nuts.

Coconut-Almond Tart

10 to 12 servings

Brown Sugar Pastry
1 cup unbleached all purpose flour
½ cup (1 stick) butter, room temperature
½ cup firmly packed light brown sugar

Coconut Filling
1 cup firmly packed light brown sugar

2 extra-large eggs
1 tablespoon amaretto
¼ teaspoon salt
1½ cups sweetened flaked coconut
1½ cups (6 ounces) blanched toasted almonds, finely chopped
2 teaspoons unbleached all purpose flour
½ teaspoon baking powder

For pastry: Preheat oven to 350°F. Cream flour, butter and sugar until smooth. Gather into ball. Wrap in plastic and refrigerate 15 minutes.

Roll dough out between 2 sheets of waxed paper into circle ⅛ inch thick. Carefully remove top sheet of paper, using long spatula to separate dough from paper if necessary. Invert dough into 11-inch tart pan with removable bottom. Carefully remove remaining paper. Press dough into pan; trim and form edges. Refrigerate 15 minutes.

Set pan on baking sheet. Bake until shell begins to brown, 10 minutes.

For filling: Whisk sugar, eggs, liqueur and salt until well blended. Stir in coconut, almonds, flour and baking powder. Pour mixture into tart shell. Bake tart until brown, 17 to 20 minutes. Cool completely before serving.

Cassis Linzer Tart

Whipped cream spiked with slivovitz lends perfect balance to this pleasantly sweet black currant tart.

8 to 10 servings

1 cup sugar
Pinch of salt
1 cup (2 sticks) well-chilled unsalted butter, cut into small pieces
2 egg yolks
2½ cups finely ground toasted hazelnuts
2 cups all purpose flour
2 teaspoons grated lemon peel
1 teaspoon vanilla
½ teaspoon cinnamon

¼ teaspoon freshly grated nutmeg
Pinch of ground cloves

2⅓ cups black currant preserves (preferably imported)
1 egg white beaten with 1 teaspoon water (glaze)

2 cups well-chilled whipping cream
3 tablespoons slivovitz* or Cognac
Powdered sugar

Combine sugar and salt in large bowl. Cut in butter until coarse meal forms. Mix in yolks. Cut in hazelnuts and flour ½ cup at a time, using pastry blender or dough hook. Add lemon peel, vanilla, cinnamon, nutmeg and cloves. Blend just until dough forms ball. Flatten dough into disc. Wrap tightly and refrigerate at least 3 hours. (*Can be prepared 1 day ahead.*)

Position rack in lower third of oven and preheat to 400°F. Roll dough out between sheets of waxed paper to ¼-inch-thick round. Transfer to 11-inch tart pan with removable bottom. Trim and finish edges. Reserve excess dough. Spread preserves in tart. Roll reserved dough out ¼ inch thick between sheets of waxed paper. Cut into ½-inch-wide strips using fluted cutter. Arrange atop filling, spacing 1 inch apart and forming lattice. Brush strips with glaze (do not drip on preserves). Set tart on baking sheet and bake 15 minutes. Reduce temperature to 350°F. Continue baking until pastry is brown and filling bubbles, about 25 minutes. Cool on wire rack 15 minutes. Remove pan rim wire and cool tart completely on rack.

Whip cream to soft peaks. Add slivovitz and 2 tablespoons powdered sugar and beat until peaks hold shape. Dust tart with additional powdered sugar. Accompany with whipped cream.

*Plum eau-de-vie imported from Yugoslavia, available at liquor stores.

Marshall Islands Macadamia Nut Pie

8 servings

2 cups macadamia nuts,
   coarsely chopped
1/3 cup shredded coconut
1 unbaked 9-inch pie crust
4 eggs, beaten to blend
1 cup light corn syrup

1/2 cup sugar
1 1/2 teaspoons vanilla
1/4 teaspoon salt

1 cup whipping cream
3 tablespoons cream of coconut

If macadamia nuts are salted, place in colander and rinse with hot water. Drain well; dry thoroughly with paper towels.

Preheat oven to 350°F. Press coconut into bottom and sides of unbaked pie shell. Combine eggs, corn syrup, sugar, vanilla and salt in large bowl and mix well. Fold in macadamia nuts. Pour into prepared pie shell. Bake 15 minutes. Reduce oven temperature to 325°F and continue baking until top is brown and filling is set, about 30 more minutes. Let pie cool.

Whip cream to soft peaks. Fold in cream of coconut. Slice pie into wedges and serve, passing coconut cream separately.

Pine Nut Tart

6 servings

Crust
1 1/3 cups all purpose flour
11 tablespoons unsalted butter,
   room temperature
1/2 teaspoon salt
1 tablespoon dark rum
1 1/4 teaspoons vanilla

Pine Nut Filling
1 cup whipping cream

2/3 cup sugar
2 1/2 teaspoons dark rum or brandy
2 1/4 teaspoons vanilla
1 2/3 cups lightly toasted pine nuts

Chocolate leaves

For crust: Preheat oven to 400°F. Blend first 3 ingredients in processor until coarse meal forms, using on/off turns. With machine running, pour rum and vanilla through feed tube and process until just combined; do not form ball. Gather dough into ball and flatten into rectangle. Wrap in plastic and refrigerate for 20 minutes.

Reserve 1 tablespoon dough. Roll remainder out between 2 sheets of waxed paper to 10 × 14-inch rectangle. Transfer to 8 × 12-inch tart pan with removable sides, discarding paper. Build crust sides up 1/8 inch above pan rim. Repair any cracks or thin spots in crust by smoothing. Refrigerate 20 minutes.

Preheat oven to 400°F. Bake crust until golden brown, about 25 minutes.

Meanwhile, prepare filling: Mix first 4 ingredients in medium bowl until sugar dissolves. Stir in nuts.

Let crust cool on rack 5 minutes. Repair any cracks by gently smoothing in reserved dough. Cool completely.

Line lower oven rack with foil, position second rack in center of oven and preheat to 350°F. Pour filling into cooled crust. Place tart on middle rack and bake until filling is deep golden brown, about 55 minutes. Immediately remove pan sides. Cool tart completely on rack. (*Can be prepared 1 day ahead.*) Serve at room temperature, garnished with chocolate leaves.

Blue Ribbon Pecan Pie

6 to 8 servings

1 cup light corn syrup
1 cup firmly packed dark brown sugar
3 eggs
⅓ cup butter, melted
Dash of vanilla

Pinch of salt
1½ cups coarsely chopped pecans
1 unbaked 9-inch pie crust
16 pecan halves (garnish)
Whipped cream or ice cream

Preheat oven to 375°F. Combine first 6 ingredients in medium bowl and mix well. Stir in chopped pecans. Pour batter into pie shell. Arrange pecan halves decoratively around top of pie, spacing evenly. Bake until center is set and crust is golden brown, about 1 hour. Serve pie at room temperature with whipped cream or ice cream.

Colonial Pecan Pie

6 to 8 servings

2 cups firmly packed light brown sugar
3 tablespoons all purpose flour
¼ cup plus 2 tablespoons milk
3 eggs, room temperature
1 tablespoon cider vinegar

1 teaspoon vanilla
½ cup (1 stick) unsalted butter, melted and cooled
1½ cups uniform pecan halves
1 partially baked 9-inch pie crust

Preheat oven to 325°F. Combine sugar and flour in large bowl and mix, pressing out all lumps. Stir in milk. Beat in eggs one at a time. Mix in vinegar and vanilla. Gradually stir in butter. Fold in pecans. Pour filling into pie shell. Bake until puffed and brown, 45 to 50 minutes. Let pie cool to room temperature before slicing and serving.

Rum, Raisin and Pecan Pie

6 to 8 servings

1½ cups sugar
1 cup raisins
¾ cup half and half
½ cup (1 stick) unsalted butter
6 egg yolks, beaten to blend
1½ cups coarsely chopped pecans (about 4½ ounces)

2 tablespoons dark rum
1 tablespoon fresh lemon juice
½ teaspoon vanilla
Pinch of salt
1 partially baked 9-inch pie crust

Preheat oven to 425°F. Combine sugar, raisins, half and half and butter in heavy small saucepan and bring to simmer over medium-low heat, stirring frequently. Remove from heat. Gradually beat hot sugar mixture into yolks in large bowl. Stir in pecans, rum, lemon juice, vanilla and salt. Pour filling into pie shell. Bake 15 minutes. Reduce oven temperature to 375°F and continue baking until puffed and golden, 45 to 50 minutes. Let pie cool 30 minutes before slicing and serving.

Butter-Rum Pecan Tart

Less "gooey" than the traditional pecan pie, but just as sinfully rich.

6 servings

Pecan Crust
- ½ cup pecans
- 1¼ cups sifted unbleached all purpose flour
- 2 tablespoons sugar
- ¼ teaspoon salt
- 6 tablespoons (¾ stick) well-chilled unsalted butter, cut into pieces
- 3 to 4 tablespoons well-chilled whipping cream

Filling
- ¼ cup firmly packed dark brown sugar
- 1 egg, room temperature
- 1 egg yolk, room temperature
- ⅔ cup light corn syrup
- ⅓ cup whipping cream
- 3 tablespoons dark rum
- 3 tablespoons unsalted butter, melted
- ¼ teaspoon salt

- 1½ cups pecans, coarsely chopped
  Whipped cream (optional)

For crust: Grind pecans medium fine in processor using on/off turns. Blend in flour, sugar and salt. Cut in butter using on/off turns until mixture resembles coarse meal. With machine running, slowly add enough cream through feed tube to moisten dough; do not form ball. Gather dough together. Form into 2 balls and flatten into discs. Wrap dough tightly; refrigerate for at least 30 minutes.

Roll 1 piece of dough out between sheets of waxed paper into 9-inch round. Pat into bottom of 9-inch tart pan with removable bottom. Cut remaining dough in half. Shape 1 piece on floured surface into ½-inch-thick cylinder. Repeat with remaining dough. Fit cylinders around edge of tart pan. Press with finger to seal with lower crust and up sides of pan. Crimp edges if desired. Refrigerate pecan crust while preparing filling.

For filling: Whisk brown sugar, egg and yolk in bowl. Whisk in corn syrup and then cream, rum, butter and salt.

Position rack in upper third of oven and preheat to 325°F. Spread pecans in crust. Rewhisk filling and pour over pecans. Bake until pecans turn rich brown, about 40 minutes. Cool on rack 30 minutes. Remove pan sides. Cool tart completely. Serve with whipped cream if desired.

Oatmeal-Pecan Pie

8 servings

- 1 9-inch deep-dish pie crust

- 2 eggs, beaten to blend
- ½ cup sugar
- ½ cup firmly packed dark brown sugar
- ¾ cup light corn syrup
- ½ cup milk
- ¼ cup (½ stick) butter, melted
- 1 teaspoon vanilla
  Pinch of salt
- ¾ cup quick-cooking oats
- ½ cup flaked coconut
- 2 ounces pecan halves

Preheat oven to 350°F. Bake pie shell 10 minutes. Retain oven temperature. Meanwhile, beat eggs with sugars in large bowl of electric mixer. Mix in corn syrup, milk, melted butter, vanilla and salt. Stir in quick-cooking oats, coconut and pecans. Spoon filling into crust, spreading evenly. Bake until set, 55 to 60 minutes. Cool completely on wire rack. Serve pie at room temperature.

Sawdust Pie

8 to 10 servings

1½ cups sugar
1½ cups flaked coconut (6 ounces)
1½ cups chopped pecans (6 ounces)
1½ cups graham cracker crumbs
7 egg whites, unbeaten

1 unbaked 10-inch pie crust
Unsweetened whipped cream
1 large banana, thinly sliced

Preheat oven to 350°F. Combine sugar, coconut, pecans, graham cracker crumbs and whites in large bowl and mix well; do not beat. Turn into pie shell. Bake until filling is just set, about 35 minutes; do not overbake. Serve warm or at room temperature. Top each serving with generous dollop of whipped cream and several banana slices.

Maple-Pecan-Chocolate Tart

8 to 10 servings

Pecan Pastry
½ cup (1 stick) well-chilled unsalted butter, cut into 8 pieces
5 tablespoons cold water
2 tablespoons sugar
2 tablespoons ground pecans
1 egg yolk
½ teaspoon salt
1½ cups unbleached all purpose flour

Filling
3 ounces unsweetened chocolate
3 tablespoons unsalted butter
⅔ cup sugar

3 tablespoons water
1 teaspoon instant coffee crystals

4 eggs, room temperature
1 cup light corn syrup
1 teaspoon vanilla
½ teaspoon maple extract
Pinch of salt
2 cups coarsely chopped pecans
16 large pecan halves
Vanilla ice cream

For pastry: Coarsely chop butter in processor using on/off turns. Add water, sugar, pecans, yolk and salt and blend using 5 to 6 on/off turns. Add flour and mix just until dough comes together; do not allow dough to form ball. Gather into ball. Flatten into disc. Wrap in plastic and refrigerate at least 2 hours or overnight. (*Can be frozen up to 1 month.*)

Roll dough out on lightly floured surface into circle ⅛ inch thick. Fit into 11-inch tart pan with removable bottom. Trim edges, leaving 1-inch overhang. Fold overhang in to form double thickness on sides. Press dough into pan, extending crust ¼ inch above edge. Flute edges. Pierce bottom and sides using fork. Refrigerate tart shell for at least 30 minutes.

Position rack in center of oven and preheat to 400°F. Line shell with parchment or foil. Fill with pie weights or dried beans. Bake until shell is set, about 12 minutes. Remove paper and weights. Pierce shell again using fork. Bake until lightly browned, about 12 minutes. Cool crust completely.

For filling: Melt chocolate and butter with sugar, water and coffee crystals in double boiler over simmering water. Stir until smooth. Cool to lukewarm.

Preheat oven to 400°F. Blend eggs, corn syrup, vanilla, maple extract and salt in large bowl. Stir in chocolate mixture and chopped pecans. Pour into crust. Arrange 10 pecan halves around outside edge of tart and 6 in center. Bake until filling is puffy and set, about 25 minutes. Serve warm with ice cream.

Can be prepared 2 days ahead. Cool completely, remove from pan, wrap and refrigerate. To serve, bring to room temperature and return to pan. Place in cold oven. Turn temperature to 300°F and reheat 15 to 20 minutes.

Chocolate Pecan Pie

*A super-rich
Southern dessert.*

6 to 8 servings

5 tablespoons unsalted butter
1 ounce unsweetened chocolate
1½ cups firmly packed dark
   brown sugar
3 eggs, room temperature
1 teaspoon vanilla

Pinch of salt
1 partially baked 9-inch pie crust
1 cup pecan halves
1 tablespoon unsalted butter,
   melted

Preheat oven to 350°F. Melt 5 tablespoons butter and chocolate in top of double boiler over barely simmering water. Stir until smooth. Cool slightly. Whisk sugar and eggs in large bowl to combine. Add vanilla and salt. Stir in chocolate mixture. Pour into crust. Arrange pecans in concentric circles on top. Bake until filling remains firm when pie is shaken, about 35 minutes. Brush with melted butter. Serve warm.

Funny Pie

8 to 10 servings

1 cup sugar
½ cup (1 stick) butter
   or margarine, melted
2 eggs
¼ cup all purpose flour
3 tablespoons unsweetened cocoa
   powder

1 teaspoon vanilla
½ cup chopped pecans
   Whipped cream and shaved
   chocolate

Preheat oven to 350°F. Grease 8-inch pie plate. Combine sugar and butter in large bowl and mix well. Add eggs, then flour, cocoa and vanilla, blending well after each addition. Stir in pecans. Turn mixture into pie plate. Bake until set, about 20 to 25 minutes. Cool slightly. Garnish with whipped cream and shaved chocolate.

Whiffletree Chocolate Chip Pie

6 to 8 servings

1 cup solid vegetable shortening
½ cup firmly packed brown sugar
½ cup sugar
1 teaspoon vanilla
2 eggs
2 cups all purpose flour
1 teaspoon baking soda

1 teaspoon salt
2 cups semisweet chocolate chips
1 cup chopped walnuts
1 unbaked 9-inch deep-dish
   pie crust
   Vanilla ice cream

Preheat oven to 350°F. Cream shortening, sugars and vanilla in large bowl using electric mixer. Beat in eggs one at a time. Combine flour, baking soda and salt. Gradually blend into sugar mixture. Stir in chocolate chips and walnuts. Spoon into pie shell, mounding slightly in center. Bake until top is lightly browned, about 10 minutes. Reduce oven temperature to 250°F. Cover pie with parchment or foil. Bake until center is set to desired firmness, about 1 hour for chewy texture. Serve warm or at room temperature with vanilla ice cream.

Jackson Pie

8 to 10 servings

6 tablespoons (¾ stick) butter, room temperature
¾ cup sugar
½ cup all purpose flour
¼ cup Marsala
1 egg

1 teaspoon vanilla
⅔ cup chopped walnuts
⅔ cup chocolate chips
1 partially baked 9-inch pie crust
Vanilla ice cream or unsweetened whipped cream

Set baking sheet on center oven rack and preheat to 325°F. Cream butter with sugar in large bowl until fluffy. Blend in flour. Add Marsala, egg and vanilla and beat well. Stir in walnuts and chocolate chips. Turn into pie crust. Cover edge of pastry with foil to prevent excessive browning. Transfer pie to preheated baking sheet and bake until filling is lightly browned, about 45 to 50 minutes. Serve warm or at room temperature. Garnish with ice cream or whipped cream.

Walnut Rum Pie

8 to 10 servings

¾ cup sugar
½ cup (1 stick) butter, melted and cooled
½ cup all purpose flour
2 eggs, beaten to blend
1 cup semisweet chocolate chips

1 cup coarsely chopped walnuts
2 tablespoons dark rum
1 11-inch partially baked sweet pie crust
Unsweetened whipped cream

Preheat oven to 350°F. Combine sugar, butter, flour and eggs in medium bowl and beat until smooth. Stir in chocolate chips, nuts and rum. Turn mixture into pie shell. Bake until filling is golden, about 30 to 35 minutes. Cool pie on rack. Serve with whipped cream.

Walnut Pie

6 to 8 servings

2 eggs, separated
1 cup dark corn syrup
½ cup firmly packed light brown sugar
¼ cup (½ stick) butter, melted
1 tablespoon all purpose flour
½ teaspoon vanilla
½ teaspoon cinnamon
⅛ teaspoon salt

Pinch of cream of tartar
1 cup coarsely chopped walnuts
1 unbaked 9-inch pie crust

Whipped cream or vanilla ice cream

Preheat oven to 350°F. Beat egg yolks with rotary beater until light and lemon colored. Add syrup, brown sugar, butter, flour, vanilla, cinnamon and salt and blend well.

Beat egg whites with cream of tartar in another bowl until stiff but not dry. Fold ⅓ into yolk mixture to loosen, then fold in remainder along with ¾ cup walnuts. Turn into pie shell. Sprinkle with remaining nuts.

Bake until knife inserted in center comes out clean, about 50 minutes. Serve pie warm or at room temperature with whipped cream or ice cream.

Deux Cheminées Walnut Tart

8 servings

Crust
1¼ cups all purpose flour
1 tablespoon sugar
½ teaspoon salt
½ cup (1 stick) well-chilled unsalted butter, cut into ½-inch pieces
1 egg yolk
3 to 4 tablespoons ice water

Filling
½ cup (1 stick) unsalted butter
2 cups firmly packed dark brown sugar

⅓ cup light corn syrup
3½ cups coarsely chopped walnuts (14 ounces)
½ cup whipping cream
1 tablespoon dark rum

Unsweetened whipped cream (optional)

For crust: Combine flour, sugar and salt in large bowl. Add butter and blend until mixture resembles coarse meal. Add yolk and ice water and mix just until dough holds together. Form dough into ball; flatten into disc. Dust lightly with flour. Wrap in plastic and refrigerate 1 hour.

Position rack in lower third of oven and preheat to 400°F. Roll dough out on lightly floured surface into 12-inch circle. Fit into 10½-inch tart pan, trimming excess. Prick bottom and sides of crust with fork. Line with foil and fill with dried beans, rice or pie weights. Bake until set, about 8 minutes. Remove foil and weights and continue baking until crust is brown and completely baked, about 17 minutes.

For filling: Melt butter with brown sugar and corn syrup in heavy saucepan over medium-high heat. Cook, stirring frequently, until mixture registers 260°F on candy thermometer. Remove from heat. Mix in walnuts and cream (be careful; mixture may foam). Continue cooking until mixture registers 200°F on candy thermometer. Remove from heat and blend in rum. Cool filling 5 minutes, then turn into baked crust. Refrigerate tart 3 hours or overnight.

Let tart stand at room temperature 30 minutes before serving. Garnish with whipped cream if desired.

Walnut Lace Tart

8 to 10 servings

Pastry
1⅓ cups unbleached all purpose flour
1 tablespoon plus 1 teaspoon sugar
¼ teaspoon salt
¾ cup (1½ sticks) well-chilled unsalted butter, cut into ½-inch pieces
3 tablespoons ice water (or more)

Filling
1 cup whipping cream
1⅓ cups sugar
⅓ cup water

1½ teaspoons vanilla
1 egg
1 egg yolk
¼ cup (½ stick) unsalted butter, melted
1⅔ cups lightly toasted chopped walnuts

3 ounces semisweet chocolate

For pastry: Sift flour, sugar and salt into large bowl. Cut in butter until mixture resembles coarse meal. Sprinkle with 3 tablespoons ice water and stir quickly with fork until dough just holds together, adding 1 to 2 teaspoons more water if necessary. Turn dough out onto waxed paper. Pat into 5- to 6-inch disc. Sprinkle lightly with flour. Wrap tightly in waxed paper. Refrigerate at least 2 hours. (*Dough can be prepared 2 to 3 days ahead and refrigerated or frozen.*)

Butter 11-inch tart pan. Roll dough out on lightly floured surface to thickness of ⅛ inch. Gently fit dough into prepared pan, trimming and finishing edges. Crimp edges decoratively if desired. Prick bottom of dough with fork at ¼-inch intervals. Refrigerate 1 hour.

Preheat oven to 375°F. Line dough with aluminum foil or waxed paper. Fill with rice, dried beans or pie weights. Bake until set, about 7 to 8 minutes. Remove weights and foil or paper and continue baking crust until browned, about 15 to 20 minutes. Cool.

For filling: Scald cream. Combine sugar with water in heavy 1½- to 2-quart saucepan and cook over low heat until dissolved, swirling pan occasionally. Increase heat to medium-high and cook until light golden brown, swirling pan occasionally. Remove from heat and gradually whisk in hot cream (be careful; hot mixture may foam up). Place over medium-low heat and cook 3 minutes. Cool 15 minutes.

Stir vanilla into caramel mixture. Whisk egg with yolk to blend, then whisk into caramel. Stir in melted butter and chopped toasted walnuts.

Position rack in center of oven and preheat to 400°F. Melt chocolate in top of double boiler over hot (but not boiling) water. Coat bottom of prepared pastry evenly with ⅔ of melted chocolate. Cool 5 minutes to set. Pour caramel filling evenly over chocolate. Place tart on large baking sheet. Bake 15 minutes. Reduce oven temperature to 375°F and continue baking 15 minutes. Cool on wire rack for about 30 minutes.

Rewarm remaining chocolate over hot (but not boiling) water. Spoon chocolate into pastry bag fitted with small writing tip or into paper cone. Pipe over surface of tart, forming lacy design. Serve at room temperature.

Walnut Fudge Tart

A sensational chocolate and nut confection that can be baked and frozen (without ganache) one month ahead. Ganache can be prepared three weeks ahead and refrigerated until ready to use.

10 to 12 servings

Ganache
- 2 cups whipping cream
- 1 pound semisweet chocolate, cut or shaved into very small pieces

Sugar Dough
- 1 cup plus 2 tablespoons (2¼ sticks) butter, room temperature
- ½ cup plus 2 tablespoons sugar
- 2 eggs
- 3 cups plus 2 tablespoons pastry flour
- Pinch of salt

Caramel Filling
- 2½ cups sugar
- 1 cup plus 3 tablespoons water
- ¼ teaspoon cream of tartar
- ¾ cup whipping cream, room temperature
- 12 ounces walnuts, coarsely chopped
- 14 tablespoons (1¾ sticks) butter, cut into small pieces

- 1 egg, beaten to blend

- ¾ cup toasted sliced almonds

For ganache: Bring whipping cream to rapid boil in medium saucepan over medium-high heat. Meanwhile, place chocolate pieces in medium bowl. Pour hot cream over chocolate in slow steady stream, stirring constantly until chocolate is melted and mixture is well blended. Refrigerate until well chilled.

For dough: Cream butter with sugar in large bowl until light and fluffy. Add eggs one at a time, beating well after each addition. Add flour and salt and stir until well mixed. (Dough will be quite thick and soft.) Wrap dough in plastic and chill at least 30 minutes.

For filling: Combine sugar, water and cream of tartar in medium saucepan, swirling to mix. Bring to boil over high heat and cook without stirring until syrup is rich medium brown and candy thermometer registers 334°F, washing down any crystals on sides of pan with brush dipped in cold water. Remove from heat and let stand 15 seconds. Add whipping cream (mixture will bubble up), swirling saucepan gently until foam subsides; *do not stir.* Mix in walnuts, stirring gently. Place butter pieces over mixture and let melt, about 5 minutes. Gently stir in melted butter until just combined. Transfer mixture to large bowl and let cool (or place bowl in ice water and stir until cool).

To assemble: Divide dough in half. Roll half of dough into circle ⅜ inch thick. Press into 9 × 1½-inch round cake pan or 10 × 1-inch tart pan with sloping sides, allowing slight overlap. Pour caramel filling over dough to ¾ full. Brush edges of pastry with beaten egg. Roll remaining dough into circle ⅜ inch thick and arrange over caramel. Roll across pastry with rolling pin to seal edges completely; trim excess pastry. Chill tart 5 minutes before baking.

Position rack in lower third of oven and preheat to 400°F. Bake tart until golden brown, about 40 to 45 minutes. Invert onto baking sheet. If too light in color (tart should be light golden on bottom), return to pan and bake 5 to 10 more minutes. Invert onto serving platter and let cool completely. Bring ganache to room temperature.

Transfer ganache to medium saucepan and swirl over medium heat to remove any chill, about 5 seconds; then pour over cooled tart, letting ganache run over sides. Using spatula, touch up any unglazed areas on sides of tart by gently lifting small amount of ganache from platter and barely pressing onto unglazed area. Carefully press nuts around sides of tart and refrigerate. Let tart stand at room temperature for 30 minutes before serving.

French Coconut Pie

8 to 10 servings

1 unbaked 9-inch pie crust
1 egg white, beaten to blend

3 eggs
1½ cups sugar
½ cup (1 stick) butter, melted

1 teaspoon vanilla
1 cup coconut
1 cup diced walnuts
Vanilla ice cream

Preheat oven to 400°F. Brush pie shell with enough egg white to coat. Bake 1 minute. Set aside. Retain oven temperature.

Beat eggs and sugar in medium bowl until smooth. Add butter and vanilla and blend well. Stir in coconut and walnuts. Turn into pie shell. Bake 10 minutes. Reduce oven temperature to 350°F and continue baking until filling is set and top is browned, about 35 minutes. Serve pie warm or at room temperature with vanilla ice cream.

Six-Nut Tart

8 servings

Nut Crust
- ½ cup finely ground almonds
- ½ cup finely ground hazelnuts
- ½ cup powdered sugar
- ¼ cup (½ stick) unsalted butter, room temperature
- ⅔ cup cake flour
- 1 egg yolk

Filling
- ¼ cup (½ stick) unsalted butter, room temperature
- 1 cup firmly packed brown sugar
- ⅓ cup light corn syrup
- 3 eggs
- 1 tablespoon brandy
- ½ teaspoon vanilla

- 1 cup mixed nuts (pecan halves, walnut halves, hazelnuts, macadamia nuts, almonds and pistachios)
- Whipped cream

For crust: Combine almonds, hazelnuts and powdered sugar in processor using on/off turns. Cream butter in large bowl using electric mixer. Blend in nut mixture and flour. Mix in yolk. Refrigerate 1 hour.

Roll dough out on lightly floured surface to 11-inch circle. Fit into 9-inch tart pan with removable bottom; trim edges. Refrigerate for 30 minutes.

Preheat oven to 350°F. Line bottom of pie shell with foil and fill with pie weights or dried beans. Bake until set, about 10 minutes. Remove weights and foil and set crust aside. Retain oven temperature.

For filling: Cream butter with brown sugar in large bowl using electric mixer. Blend in corn syrup. Beat in eggs one at a time. Mix in brandy and vanilla.

Spread mixed nuts on baking sheet. Toast until golden, about 10 minutes. Increase oven temperature to 375°F. Arrange half of nuts in bottom of crust. Pour in filling. Decorate with remaining nuts. Bake until filling is set and crust is crisp, about 40 minutes (if edges brown too quickly, cover loosely with foil). Cool to room temperature before serving. Top with whipped cream.

Nuss Tart

8 to 10 servings

Walnut Filling
- 5 ounces walnuts
- ⅔ cup vanilla sugar or granulated sugar
- ⅔ cup milk
- 2 tablespoons dark rum
- ¼ teaspoon cinnamon
  Large pinch of ground cloves
  Large pinch of freshly grated nutmeg

Almond Tart Pastry
- 4 3 × ½-inch strips lemon peel, cut into ½-inch pieces
- ⅓ cup vanilla sugar or granulated sugar

- ⅔ cup whole blanched almonds
- 1¼ cups sifted all purpose flour
- ¾ cup (1½ sticks) well-chilled unsalted butter, cut into 12 pieces
- 1 egg yolk

- ⅓ cup seedless red raspberry jam

- 1 cup well-chilled whipping cream
- 3 tablespoons powdered sugar
- 1 tablespoon dark rum
  Powdered sugar

For filling: Grate walnuts in processor using medium shredding disc. Combine with remaining ingredients in small saucepan. Cook over low heat, swirling pan occasionally, until sugar dissolves. Increase heat and boil gently until mixture thickens slightly, 5 to 7 minutes. Cool completely.

For pastry: Finely mince lemon peel with ⅓ cup vanilla sugar in processor, about 1 minute. Add almonds and process 20 seconds. Add both flours and mix using 5 on/off turns. Arrange butter in circle atop flour. Process until mixture is powdery, stopping once to scrape down sides of work bowl, 10 to 15 seconds. Add yolk and process until ball forms. If not thoroughly combined, cut into 4 pieces, distribute evenly in work bowl and process 5 to 10 seconds longer.

Roll ⅓ of pastry out between sheets of waxed paper to 9-inch round; trim if necessary. (If pastry becomes too soft to work, freeze 10 to 15 minutes.) Transfer to baking sheet. Freeze while rolling remaining pastry.

Butter 9 × ¾-inch tart pan with removable bottom. Dust with flour. Roll remaining pastry out between sheets of waxed paper into 11-inch circle. Transfer to prepared pan, discarding paper. Trim and finish edges. Spread jam over pastry. Freeze to firm pastry and jam, 15 to 20 minutes.

Preheat oven to 350°F. Top jam with filling, spreading evenly. Place pastry circle atop tart, discarding paper. Let tart stand at room temperature until top softens slightly, 5 to 10 minutes. Gently press top and bottom pastry together to seal. Place tart on baking sheet. Bake until golden brown, 35 to 40 minutes. Cool in pan on rack 30 minutes. Remove pan rim. Cool tart completely. (*Can be prepared 2 days ahead and refrigerated. Bring to room temperature before serving.*)

To serve, whip cream, 3 tablespoons powdered sugar and rum in well-chilled bowl until soft peaks form. Dust tart with additional powdered sugar. Pass whipped cream separately.

Butter Tarts

Makes about 40 small tartlets

Crust
2 cups all purpose flour
Pinch of salt
⅓ cup well-chilled unsalted butter, cut into pieces
⅓ cup well-chilled lard or solid vegetable shortening
4 to 6 tablespoons ice water

Filling
½ cup raisins

¾ cup firmly packed brown sugar
¾ cup light corn syrup
2 eggs
¼ cup (½ stick) unsalted butter, room temperature
½ teaspoon vanilla

For crust: Combine flour and salt in large bowl. Cut in butter and lard until mixture resembles coarse meal. Blend in 4 tablespoons ice water and mix just until dough holds together, adding more water if necessary. Halve dough. Shape into discs. Wrap in plastic and chill while preparing filling.

For filling: Plump raisins in boiling water to cover 10 minutes. Drain and pat dry. Set aside. Mix remaining ingredients in 1-quart glass measuring cup until smooth. Set aside.

Roll each portion of dough out on lightly floured surface to thickness of ⅛ inch. Cut out 2-inch rounds using cookie cutter or glass. Firmly press rounds into 1¾-inch (top diameter) muffin tins. Wrap scraps in plastic and refrigerate at least 10 minutes.

Preheat oven to 400°F. Reroll scraps, cut out additional rounds and press into tins. Place 3 or 4 raisins in each tart. Pour filling into each, almost to top. Bake until filling is set, about 20 minutes. Cool 10 minutes in tins, then remove from tins by running sharp knife around edges. Cool on racks. Serve tarts at room temperature.

Buttermilk Pie

8 to 10 servings

½ cup (1 stick) butter
1½ cups sugar
2 tablespoons all purpose flour
3 eggs
½ cup buttermilk
1 teaspoon vanilla

1 baked 9-inch pie crust
1 egg white, beaten to blend

Position rack in lower third of oven and preheat to 350°F. Melt butter in small saucepan over low heat. Blend sugar and flour in large bowl. Add melted butter and mix well using wooden spoon. Add eggs one at a time, beating well with wooden spoon after each addition. Stir in buttermilk and vanilla.

Brush pastry with egg white to waterproof crust. Let dry 2 minutes. Pour in filling. Bake until filling is set, about 45 minutes. Cool at least 20 minutes. Serve warm, at room temperature or chilled.

Kentucky Chess Pie

6 to 8 servings

2 cups sugar
2 tablespoons stone-ground white cornmeal
2 tablespoons all purpose flour
3 eggs, beaten to blend
1 cup half and half

½ cup (1 stick) unsalted butter, melted and cooled
1 teaspoon vanilla
¼ teaspoon salt
1 partially baked 9-inch pie crust

Preheat oven to 425°F. Mix sugar, cornmeal and flour in large bowl. Stir in eggs. Blend in half and half, butter, vanilla and salt. Pour filling into pie shell. Bake 15 minutes. Reduce oven temperature to 375°F and continue baking until puffed and golden, 45 to 50 minutes. Let pie cool to room temperature before slicing and serving.

Brown Sugar Pie

6 to 8 servings

2 cups firmly packed light brown sugar
1½ teaspoons cornstarch
4 eggs, room temperature
3 tablespoons whipping cream

1 tablespoon fresh lemon juice
2 teaspoon vanilla
⅓ cup unsalted butter, melted and cooled
1 partially baked 9-inch pie crust

Preheat oven to 325°F. Combine brown sugar and cornstarch in large bowl and mix, pressing out any lumps. Beat in eggs one at a time. Stir in cream, lemon juice and vanilla. Blend in melted butter. Pour filling into pie shell. Bake until puffed and browned, 50 to 60 minutes. Cool to room temperature before serving. (Filling will thicken, fall somewhat and acquire jellylike texture as it cools.)

Chess Pies

Chess: What does it mean? Where did the term originate? There are several theories about the name of this favorite Southern sweet. One is that *chess* is merely *chest* with the *t* dropped as so often happens when Southerners speak. Chess pies were indeed the *chest* or "keeping" pies of plantation days, pies so sugary they didn't have to be kept in the ice house like ordinary custard pies. Some food historians insist that chess is merely a corruption of cheese, which the English call their rich-as-all-get-out lemon curd; the filling of a lemon chess pie closely resembles lemon cheese.

But the most endearing theory for the origin of the name is also the simplest: When a plantation cook was asked what she was making, she modestly replied, "Jes' pie."

Brown Sugar Coconut Pie

6 servings

1 cup light corn syrup
½ cup firmly packed dark
   brown sugar
2 tablespoons (¼ stick) butter

3 eggs, beaten until frothy
⅓ cup flaked coconut
¼ teaspoon vanilla
1 unbaked 9-inch pie crust

Preheat oven to 350°F. Combine corn syrup, brown sugar and butter in medium saucepan. Bring to boil over medium heat. Remove from heat. Add eggs in thin stream, stirring constantly. Mix in coconut and vanilla. Pour into shell. Bake until brown, 30 to 35 minutes. Serve pie warm or at room temperature.

Mystery Macaroon Pie

6 to 8 servings

3 eggs, separated
¼ teaspoon salt
1½ cups sugar
1½ cups flaked coconut
¼ cup milk
2 tablespoons (¼ stick) butter,
   melted and cooled

1 teaspoon fresh lemon juice
½ teaspoon almond extract
1 unbaked 9-inch deep-dish
   pie crust

½ cup whipping cream, whipped
½ cup toasted coconut

Preheat oven to 375°F. Beat yolks with salt in large bowl of electric mixer until thickened, about 1 minute. Add sugar in 2 additions, beating well after each. Add 1½ cups coconut, milk, butter, lemon juice and almond extract and mix well. Beat whites until stiff but not dry. Gently fold into coconut mixture. Spoon into pie shell. Bake until top is browned and center is set, about 50 minutes. Cool pie completely.

Just before serving, garnish with whipped cream and toasted coconut.

Orange-Coconut Chess Pie

Makes two 9-inch pies

½ cup (1 stick) butter,
room temperature
2 cups sugar
5 eggs
½ cup thawed frozen orange
juice concentrate

⅓ cup water
1 tablespoon all purpose flour
1 tablespoon yellow cornmeal
½ cup shredded coconut
2 unbaked 9-inch pie crusts

Preheat oven to 350°F. Cream butter in large bowl of electric mixer. Gradually add sugar and beat well. Beat in eggs one at a time. Combine orange juice concentrate and water and blend into butter mixture. Beat in flour and cornmeal. Fold in coconut. Divide mixture evenly between pie shells. Bake until golden, about 50 to 60 minutes. Let pies cool before serving.

Lemon-Raisin Chess Pie

8 servings

1 cup boiling water
½ cup raisins

¼ cup (½ stick) butter
1 cup sugar
2 eggs
2 tablespoons fresh lemon juice

1 teaspoon vanilla
Finely grated peel of 1 lemon

1 baked 8-inch pie crust
1 egg white, beaten to blend

Pour boiling water over raisins and let stand about 30 minutes to plump.

Meanwhile, cream butter with sugar. Add eggs and beat well. Add lemon juice, vanilla and peel and mix well (lemon juice will cause filling mixture to have curdled appearance).

Position rack in lower third of oven and preheat to 350°F. Brush pastry with egg white to waterproof crust. Let dry 2 minutes. Drain raisins and stir into filling. Pour into pastry. Bake until filling is firm and golden brown, about 45 minutes (if pie begins to brown too quickly, reduce oven temperature to 325°F). Serve at room temperature or refrigerate pie and serve chilled.

Lemon Chess Pie

6 to 8 servings

1½ cups sugar
4 teaspoons cornstarch
2 teaspoons finely grated
lemon peel
4 eggs, room temperature

⅓ cup fresh lemon juice
5 tablespoons unsalted butter,
melted and cooled
1 partially baked 9-inch pie crust

Preheat oven to 375°F. Combine sugar and cornstarch in large bowl and mix, pressing out any lumps. Stir in lemon peel. Beat in eggs one at a time. Stir in lemon juice. Blend in butter. Pour filling into pie shell. Bake until puffed and golden brown, 50 to 60 minutes. Cool to room temperature before serving. (Filling will thicken, fall somewhat and acquire jellylike texture as it cools.)

Lemon Chess Tart

8 servings

Pâte Sablée

⅔ cup almond meal (finely ground blanched almonds)
⅔ cup sifted powdered sugar
11 tablespoons unsalted butter, room temperature
1 egg
2 teaspoons finely grated lemon peel
Pinch of salt
1½ cups plus 2 tablespoons pastry flour or all purpose flour

Melted butter

¼ cup whipping cream
1 tablespoon yellow cornmeal
½ cup (1 stick) unsalted butter, room temperature
1 cup (scant) sugar
3 eggs, room temperature
1 teaspoon finely grated lemon peel
1 teaspoon fresh lemon juice
⅛ to ¼ teaspoon lemon extract (optional)
2 to 3 tablespoons powdered sugar
Whipped cream (optional)

For pâte sablée: Mix almond meal and powdered sugar in processor to fine powder, about 10 seconds. Transfer to bowl of electric mixer. Add butter and beat until light. Blend in egg, lemon peel and salt. Beat in flour all at once until just combined; do not overmix. Gather dough into ball. Wrap in plastic and refrigerate at least 3 hours.

Roll dough out on generously floured surface into 11½-inch circle ⅛ inch thick. (Keep surface and rolling pin well floured to prevent sticking.) Fit dough into 10-inch tart pan; trim edges. Cover with plastic wrap and refrigerate for at least 1 hour.

Preheat oven to 400°F. Brush shiny side of 11½-inch foil circle lightly with melted butter. Fit buttered side down into shell. Fill with dried beans or pie weights. Bake until dough is set, 15 to 20 minutes. Remove foil and weights. Continue baking shell until golden brown, about 5 minutes. Reduce oven temperature to 350°F.

Stir cream into cornmeal in small bowl. Cream butter and sugar in bowl of electric mixer until light and fluffy. Beat in eggs one at a time and continue beating until light. Blend in cornmeal mixture, lemon peel, juice and extract.

Spoon filling into shell almost to rim; do not overfill. Bake tart until custard is set, about 30 minutes. (If edges brown too quickly, cover with strips of foil.) Cool on rack. Just before serving, dust tart lightly with powdered sugar. Garnish with whipped cream if desired.

Tidewater Peanut Pie

6 to 8 servings

¾ cup smooth peanut butter
½ cup (1 stick) unsalted butter
1 cup sugar
1 cup firmly packed light brown sugar
3 eggs

2 tablespoons all purpose flour
⅓ cup light corn syrup
⅓ cup milk or evaporated milk
1 teaspoon vanilla
Pinch of salt
1 partially baked 9-inch pie crust

Preheat oven to 325°F. Melt peanut butter and butter in heavy small saucepan over low heat, stirring occasionally. Remove mixture from heat. Combine sugar, brown sugar, eggs, flour, corn syrup, milk, vanilla and salt in large bowl and mix well. Blend in peanut butter mixture. Pour filling into pie shell. Bake until filling is puffed, about 1 hour and 20 minutes; filling will still be quite soft. Let pie cool to room temperature before slicing and serving.

❦ *Chocolate Chess and Brownie Pies*

Chocolate Chess Pie

Top this fudgelike pie with vanilla ice cream or a drift of whipped cream.

8 servings

1½ cups sugar
5 tablespoons Dutch process cocoa
2 tablespoons all purpose flour
¼ teaspoon salt
½ cup evaporated milk

3 eggs, room temperature
⅓ cup unsalted butter, melted and cooled
1 teaspoon vanilla
1 partially baked 9-inch pie crust

Preheat oven to 325°F. Combine sugar, cocoa, flour and salt in large bowl and mix well, pressing out any lumps. Blend in milk. Beat in eggs one at a time. Add butter and vanilla and beat until smooth. Pour filling into pie shell. Bake until filling is puffed and set, 55 to 60 minutes. Let pie cool to room temperature before serving.

Elizabeth's Light Chess Pie with Chocolate and Raspberries

A somewhat less sweet version of the traditional Southern favorite.

6 servings

3 extra-large eggs, separated, room temperature
¾ cup sugar
⅓ cup sour cream
¼ cup cake flour
1½ tablespoons fresh lemon juice
½ teaspoon vanilla
Pinch of cream of tartar
1 baked deep-dish 9-inch pie crust

2 tablespoons (¼ stick) butter
2 teaspoons dark rum
¼ cup semisweet chocolate chips

1 ounce semisweet chocolate

½ pint fresh raspberries or halved strawberries
1 cup whipping cream, whipped

Preheat oven to 375°F. Blend yolks in large bowl of electric mixer. Gradually add sugar and beat until pale yellow and ribbon forms when beaters are lifted. Blend in sour cream, flour, lemon juice and vanilla. Beat whites with cream of tartar in another bowl until stiff but not dry. Gently fold ¼ of whites into yolk mixture to lighten, then fold in remaining whites. Pour mixture into crust. Bake until center puffs and browns, 17 to 19 minutes. Let cool completely on wire rack (center of pie will fall as it cools).

Heat butter and rum in heavy small saucepan until butter melts. Remove from heat and stir in chocolate chips until smooth. Spread evenly over pie. Cool until chocolate sets.

Shave 1 ounce semisweet chocolate onto waxed paper using vegetable peeler. Refrigerate until chilled.

Just before serving, top pie with berries. Pipe whipped cream decoratively over berries and crust. Sprinkle top of pie with shaved chocolate.

Colonial Innkeeper's Pie

8 to 10 servings

1½ ounces unsweetened chocolate
½ cup water
⅔ cup sugar
8 tablespoons (1 stick) butter, room temperature
2 teaspoons vanilla

1 cup all purpose flour
¾ cup sugar

1 teaspoon baking powder
½ teaspoon salt
½ cup milk
1 egg
1 unbaked 9-inch pie crust
½ cup chopped walnuts
1 cup whipping cream, whipped

Preheat oven to 350°F. Melt chocolate with water in small saucepan over hot water, stirring frequently. Add ⅔ cup sugar. Remove from over water, place directly over medium-high heat and bring to boil, stirring constantly. Remove from heat. Add 4 tablespoons butter and stir until melted. Add 1½ teaspoons vanilla. Set aside.

Combine flour, ¾ cup sugar, baking powder and salt in medium bowl of electric mixer. Add milk and remaining butter and vanilla and beat 2 minutes. Add egg and beat 2 more minutes. Pour batter into pie shell. Stir chocolate sauce and carefully pour over batter. Sprinkle with nuts. Bake until tester inserted in center comes out clean, about 55 minutes. Serve pie warm or at room temperature with whipped cream.

Aunt Catfish's Boatsinker

8 servings

10 tablespoons (1¼ sticks) unsalted butter
⅓ cup dark corn syrup
2½ ounces unsweetened chocolate

1 cup sugar
3 eggs
1 teaspooon vanilla

¼ teaspoon salt
1 partially baked 9-inch deep-dish pie crust

Extra-rich coffee ice cream
Magic Shell ice cream topping
Whipped cream and maraschino cherries

Preheat oven to 325°F. Combine butter, corn syrup and chocolate in top of double boiler and melt over gently simmering water until smooth. Cool to lukewarm.

Beat sugar, eggs, vanilla and salt in medium bowl until creamy. Blend in chocolate mixture. Turn into pie shell. Bake 15 minutes. Reduce oven temperature to 275°F and continue baking until tester inserted in center comes out clean, about 30 to 35 minutes. Let pie cool on wire rack.

To serve, cut pie into 8 wedges. Top each with 2 scoops of ice cream. Drizzle topping over ice cream to coat. Garnish with whipped cream and cherries.

Double Chocolate Tart

This tart is dense and brownielike. Serve warm or at room temperature.

8 servings

Crust

1½ ounces almond or hazelnut macaroons
  1 cup unbleached all purpose flour
  1 tablespoon sugar
    Pinch of salt
  6 tablespoons (¾ stick) unsalted butter, cut into 6 pieces and frozen
2½ to 3 tablespoons ice water

Filling

  ½ cup (1 stick) unsalted butter, cut into 8 pieces
  2 ounces unsweetened chocolate, coarsely chopped

  1 cup sugar
  2 eggs
  ½ teaspoon vanilla
    Pinch of salt
  ½ cup all purpose flour

  ¼ cup strained raspberry jam or orange marmalade

Topping

  3 ounces semisweet chocolate, coarsely chopped
  ½ ounce unsweetened chocolate, coarsely chopped
  3 to 4 tablespoons water or coffee
    Powdered sugar (optional)

For crust: Preheat oven to 400°F. Place macaroons on baking sheet and bake until dry, about 5 minutes, watching carefully. Grind to fine crumbs in processor. Measure ¼ cup and return to processor. Mix in flour, sugar and salt. Blend in butter using on/off turns until mixture resembles coarse meal. Add 2½ tablespoons ice water and mix 15 seconds using on/off turns. Pinch small piece of mixture: If it sticks together, continue; if dry and crumbly, add remaining ½ tablespoon water. Continue blending dough using on/off turns until wreath of dough forms on top of blade (do not form ball). Gather into ball; flatten into disc.

Flour dough lightly. Roll dough out into 14-inch circle between sheets of waxed paper. Peel off waxed paper and roll dough up on rolling pin. Unroll into unbuttered 9-inch quiche pan with removable bottom. Trim and finish edges. Line crust with buttered foil. Fill with dried beans or pie weights. Bake 10 minutes. Remove beans and foil. Continue baking crust until golden brown, 4 to 5 minutes. Cool completely on wire rack.

For filling: Preheat oven to 350°F. Melt ¼ cup butter with chocolate in top of double boiler over hot (but not boiling) water. Remove from over water and stir until smooth. Cream remaining ¼ cup butter and sugar in processor until light and fluffy. Mix in eggs, vanilla and salt. Blend in chocolate mixture, stopping occasionally to scrape down sides of work bowl. Mix in flour in batches.

Spread jam over bottom of cooled crust. Pour in chocolate mixture. Bake until knife inserted in center comes out clean, about 25 minutes. Cool on rack until warm, about 15 minutes.

For topping: Melt semisweet chocolate, unsweetened chocolate and water in top of double boiler over hot (but not boiling) water. Remove from over water and stir until smooth. Spread atop tart. Sift powdered sugar over tart if desired. Store at room temperature.

Tart can be prepared 1 day ahead.

5 ❧ Frozen Pies

Frozen pies are a busy cook's ideal dessert: Apart from a final flourish of chocolate curls, a sprinkling of nuts or another equally simple garnish, they can be made at your convenience and slipped into the freezer to be served at a moment's notice. Best of all, their ease of preparation is deceptive, for these pies make a handsome presentation indeed.

Ice cream shows off its versatility here in a number of ways. With only three ingredients, nothing could be simpler to prepare than Sly Lemon Pie (page 110). Or dress up vanilla ice cream with peanut butter, honey and cashews for the distinctive Nut Butter Pie on page 114. And then there is luscious Kahlúa Mocha Parfait Pie (page 114), which features a coconut-pecan crust filled with mocha chip ice cream and topped with whipped cream and a splash of coffee liqueur.

Dark and White Chocolate Mousse Pie (page 112) would satisfy any chocoholic; its chocolate wafer crust encloses layers of semisweet chocolate and white chocolate-laced whipped cream. Equally sensational is Frozen White Chocolate Pie with Raspberries (page 112), in which toasted almonds form the crust for a liqueur-spiked filling. Either dessert makes the perfect rich but cooling finale to a special dinner.

A few hints will prove helpful for all of these pies. Be sure to wrap them well for freezing so that they don't pick up flavors from other foods. Before serving, transfer the pie to the refrigerator for 10 to 15 minutes to soften slightly. And keep in mind that a knife dipped in hot water and wiped dry will make slicing a lot easier . . . a real plus, because with desserts this delicious you can expect a lot of requests for seconds.

Sly Lemon Pie

6 to 8 servings

1 quart vanilla ice cream, softened
1 6-ounce can frozen lemonade
   concentrate, thawed

1 baked 9-inch pie crust
Sliced lemon twists

Combine ice cream and lemonade in blender or processor until smooth. Pour into pie shell. Freeze until firm, about 1½ hours. Let stand 10 minutes before serving. Garnish with lemon twists.

Lemon Freezer Pie

12 servings

1½ cups vanilla wafer crumbs

3 eggs, separated
½ cup sugar

1 cup whipping cream, whipped
¼ cup fresh lemon juice

Butter 9 × 9-inch metal baking pan. Press ¾ cup crumbs into bottom. Reserve remainder. Chill crust while preparing filling.

Beat whites in large bowl of electric mixer until frothy. Gradually add sugar and continue beating until soft peaks form. Add yolks one at a time, beating well after each addition. Fold in whipped cream and lemon juice. Pour into prepared crust. Sprinkle remaining ¾ cup crumbs over top. Freeze overnight before serving.

Lemon Torte

8 to 10 servings

Crust
1 5½-ounce package lemon crunch
   cookies, finely crushed
6 tablespoons (¾ stick)
   butter, melted

Lemon Filling
4 eggs, separated
1 cup sugar

½ cup fresh lemon juice
1½ tablespoons finely grated
   lemon peel
1½ cups whipping cream, whipped

1 10-ounce package frozen
   raspberries, thawed

For crust: Combine crushed cookies and butter in medium bowl and blend well. Pat onto bottom and sides of 8½-inch springform pan. Refrigerate.

For filling: Beat egg whites at medium speed of electric mixer until foamy. Gradually add sugar, beating constantly until stiff peaks form. Beat yolks in another bowl until thick and lemon colored. Stir in lemon juice and peel. Gently fold egg whites into yolks, blending well. Gently fold in cream. Pour mixture into crust and freeze.

Puree raspberries in processor or blender. Strain into serving bowl.

Let torte stand at room temperature 10 minutes before serving. Remove springform. Transfer torte to platter and serve immediately with pureed raspberries.

Orange-Lemon Ice Cream Pie

6 to 8 servings

Crust
1 cup whipping cream
2 tablespoons sugar
1 teaspoon vanilla

Filling
2 cups whipping cream

1 cup sugar
1/3 cup orange liqueur
   Finely grated peel of 1 lemon

1 cup whipping cream, whipped

For crust: Combine cream, sugar and vanilla in small bowl and beat until stiff. Turn into 9-inch pie plate, spreading evenly over bottom and sides. Freeze.

   For filling: Combine cream, sugar, liqueur and lemon peel in medium bowl, stirring constantly until sugar is dissolved. Turn into crust and freeze until set.

   Just before serving, pipe remaining whipped cream over pie.

Orange Sherbet Pie

8 to 10 servings

1/2 cup (1 stick) butter
1 7-ounce package flaked coconut
1/2 gallon orange sherbet, softened
1 to 2 tablespoons orange liqueur
   or to taste

Fresh mint leaves, strips of orange peel and mandarin orange segments

Melt butter in large skillet over medium heat. Add coconut and cook, stirring constantly, until golden, about 6 to 7 minutes. Remove from heat. Reserve 2 tablespoons coconut for garnish. Press remainder into bottom and sides of 9-inch pie plate. Spread half of orange sherbet over crust. Drizzle with liqueur. Add remaining sherbet, mounding top. Sprinkle with reserved coconut. Freeze until ready to serve, or overnight. Let stand 10 to 15 minutes before serving. Garnish with mint, orange peel and mandarin orange segments.

Frozen Orange-Coconut Pie

8 servings

Coconut Crust
3 tablespoons unsalted butter
1 ounce unsweetened chocolate
1 tablespoon whipping cream
1 teaspoon instant coffee powder
1/2 cup powdered sugar
1/2 teaspoon vanilla
1/2 teaspoon almond extract
1/4 teaspoon cinnamon
7 ounces flaked toasted coconut

1 14-ounce can sweetened condensed milk

3 1/2 tablespoons fresh lemon juice
1/2 cup orange marmalade
1 teaspoon vanilla
1 teaspoon orange extract
1 1/2 cups whipping cream, whipped

1 large orange, peeled and thinly sliced
2 1.65-ounce chocolate-coconut candy bars, chopped

For crust: Generously grease 9-inch deep-dish pie plate. Melt butter and chocolate in medium saucepan over low heat. Stir in cream and coffee powder and mix until smooth. Add powdered sugar, vanilla, almond extract and cinnamon and blend well. Remove from heat and fold in coconut. Press mixture into bottom and sides of prepared pie dish. Refrigerate while preparing filling.

Mix milk and lemon juice in large bowl. Stir in marmalade, vanilla and orange extract. Fold in whipped cream. Spoon into crust. Freeze overnight.

Remove pie from freezer 10 to 15 minutes before serving. Garnish with orange and candy.

Frozen White Chocolate Pie with Raspberries

8 servings

Almond Crust
- 9 ounces (1¾ cups) blanched toasted almonds
- 3 tablespoons unsalted butter, melted
- 2 tablespoons light corn syrup

Filling
- 10 ounces white chocolate, coarsely chopped
- 3 tablespoons unsalted butter
- ⅓ cup evaporated milk
- 3 tablespoons crème de cacao
- 1½ teaspoons vanilla
- ¼ teaspoon almond extract
- 1¾ cups whipping cream
- 2 egg whites, room temperature
- 2 tablespoons sugar
- 1¼ cups raspberries or strawberries
- Dark chocolate leaves

For crust: Grease 9-inch glass pie plate. Using heavy knife, chop almonds into 2 to 3 pieces each. Transfer almonds to bowl. Stir in butter and corn syrup. Spoon into prepared plate. Press onto bottom and up sides of plate. Freeze.

For filling: Melt chocolate and butter with milk in double boiler over gently simmering water, stirring until smooth. Remove from over water and set in bowl filled with water and ice. Let cool until thick and pastelike, stirring occasionally. Blend in liqueur, vanilla and extract. Beat cream until stiff peaks form. Gently beat in chocolate mixture. Using clean dry beaters, beat whites until soft peaks form. Add sugar 1 tablespoon at a time and beat until stiff but not dry. Fold gently into chocolate-cream mixture. Pour into crust, smoothing top. Freeze until frozen but not hard, about 5 hours.

Mound raspberries in center of pie, leaving 2-inch border. Arrange chocolate leaves around border and serve.

Dark and White Chocolate Mousse Pie

6 to 8 servings

Chocolate Crust
- 6 ounces chocolate wafers
- ⅓ cup pecans
- ¼ cup (½ stick) well-chilled butter, cut into 4 pieces

Filling
- 10 ounces semisweet chocolate
- 4 eggs, separated, room temperature
- ¼ cup coffee liqueur
- ½ cup whipping cream
- 1 ounce white chocolate, grated

For crust: Generously butter 10-inch pie pan. Grind wafers, pecans and butter in processor to coarse meal. Press into bottom and sides of pan.

For filling: Melt semisweet chocolate in top of double boiler set over gently simmering water. Remove from over water. Blend in yolks and coffee liqueur. Transfer to large bowl. Beat whites in another large bowl until stiff but not dry. Fold into chocolate mixture in 3 batches. Beat cream in medium bowl until stiff peaks form. Blend in grated white chocolate.

Fill shell with half of semisweet chocolate mixture. Top with whipped cream mixture. Spoon remaining semisweet chocolate mixture over, spreading evenly. Freeze at least 30 minutes before serving.

Bountiful Hot Fudge Sundae Pie

10 to 12 servings

Chocolate Cookie Crumb Crust
1¼ cups fine chocolate wafer crumbs
  ¼ cup finely ground toasted nuts
      (almonds, hazelnuts or walnuts)
  3 tablespoons sugar
  6 tablespoons (¾ stick) unsalted
      butter, melted

Hot Fudge Sauce
  1 cup sugar
  ¾ cup unsweetened cocoa powder,
      sifted
  1 teaspoon instant coffee powder

  1 cup whipping cream
  ¼ cup (½ stick) unsalted butter

Filling
  1 quart rich vanilla ice cream,
      softened
  1 quart rich chocolate ice cream,
      frozen
  ½ cup whipping cream, whipped
      Coarsely chopped toasted nuts
      Maraschino cherries (with
      stems), rinsed and drained

For crust: Combine crumbs, nuts and sugar in small bowl and mix well. Pour melted butter over mixture and toss lightly until well blended. Press mixture evenly onto bottom and sides of 9- to 10-inch pie plate. Cover with plastic wrap and chill 30 minutes.

For sauce: Combine sugar, cocoa and instant coffee in medium saucepan. Add ½ cup whipping cream and blend to smooth paste. Add remaining cream, blending well. Cook over medium heat, stirring constantly, until sugar is completely dissolved. Add butter and cook until mixture is smooth and thickened, about 5 to 8 minutes. Keep warm. (*Can be prepared ahead, covered and refrigerated. Reheat before using.*)

For filling: Spread half of softened vanilla ice cream evenly over crust and freeze. Drizzle half of hot fudge sauce over top (fudge will solidify). Spread remaining vanilla ice cream over fudge. Return to freezer to firm.

Scoop balls from chocolate ice cream and arrange over vanilla layer. Drizzle with remaining hot fudge. Spoon whipped cream into pastry bag fitted with star tip and pipe rosettes around scoops. Decorate with nuts and cherries. Serve pie immediately.

Coffee-Chocolate Jewel Pie

8 servings

  1 pint coffee ice cream, slightly
      softened
  1 baked 8-inch chocolate
      wafer crust
  ¼ cup semisweet chocolate chips

  ¼ cup marshmallow creme
  ¼ cup fudge sauce
  ¼ cup chopped pecans
      Whipped cream

Spread half of ice cream in pie crust. Sprinkle with half of chips. Spoon marshmallow creme over chips. Spread remaining ice cream over marshmallow creme. Pour fudge sauce over. Sprinkle with pecans and remaining chocolate chips. Freeze pie. Let stand at room temperature about 10 minutes before serving. Top slices with whipped cream.

Kahlúa Mocha Parfait Pie

8 servings

7 ounces sweetened flaked coconut
4 ounces pecans, finely chopped
2 tablespoons all purpose flour
½ cup (1 stick) butter, melted

3 pints mocha chip ice cream, slightly softened

Whipped cream
Grated semisweet chocolate
1 cup Kahlúa

Preheat oven to 375°F. Combine coconut, pecans and flour in large bowl. Blend in melted butter. Press mixture into bottom and sides of 10-inch metal pie pan. Bake until golden brown, about 10 minutes. Cool crust completely.

Pack ice cream into crust. Freeze until firm. Top with whipped cream. Sprinkle with grated chocolate. Cut pie into 8 wedges. Pour 2 tablespoons Kahlúa over each and serve immediately.

Kennebunk Inn Sno-Pie

8 to 10 servings

2 cups graham cracker crumbs
6 tablespoons (¾ stick) unsalted butter, melted

3 cups (24 ounces) imitation sour cream
2 cups sifted powdered sugar

1 8¼-ounce can crushed pineapple (packed in its own juice)
½ cup cream of coconut
½ cup white rum or to taste

½ cup shredded coconut
⅓ cup chopped toasted pecans

Preheat oven to 375°F. Generously grease 8-inch springform pan. Combine crumbs and butter in medium bowl until well blended. Pat mixture evenly onto bottom and sides of prepared pan. Bake until set, about 8 minutes. Remove from oven and let cool completely.

Combine sour cream, sugar, pineapple, cream of coconut and rum in large bowl and beat at low speed of electric mixer until blended. Increase speed and continue beating 3 minutes (towel placed over bowl will prevent splattering).

Pour mixture into prepared crust. Sprinkle with coconut and nuts. Freeze until firm, about 6 hours, or overnight. Let stand at room temperature about 20 minutes before serving. Run sharp knife around crust and remove springform.

Nut Butter Pie

This sinful pie must be made and frozen at least two days ahead.

12 to 15 servings

12 ounces chocolate wafer crumbs
¼ cup sugar
¼ cup (½ stick) butter, melted

½ gallon vanilla ice cream, softened
2 cups smooth peanut butter

1 cup clover honey
1 cup chopped toasted cashews

2 cups chocolate fudge sauce, heated
2 cups whipped cream

Preheat oven to 350°F. Lightly grease 9-inch springform pan. Blend chocolate crumbs, sugar and melted butter in medium bowl. Press onto bottom and up sides of prepared pan. Bake 5 minutes. Cool.

Mix ice cream, peanut butter, honey and cashews in large bowl. Spoon into prepared crust. Freeze at least 2 days.

Place pie in shallow pan of hot water 10 seconds. Remove pie from pan. Top each serving with sauce and whipped cream.

❧ Index

🍎 Credits and Acknowledgments

The following people contributed the recipes included in this book:

Algiers Landing, New Orleans,
   Louisiana
Jean Anderson
Aunt Catfish's, Port Orange, Florida
Aux Anciens Canadiens, Montréal
Paula Ayers
Rose Levy Beranbaum
Dale Booher
Marcia and William Bond
Anita Borghese
Jean Brady
Betty Brown
Mary Bryant
Susan Bullard
Anne Byrd
Sharon Cadwallader
George Caloyannidis
Sue Cam
Campton Place, San Francisco,
   California
Terrie Cave
Clay Hill Farm, Ogunquit, Maine
Clara Cook
Darrell Costi
Christa Craig
Creek Café, Big Rapids, Michigan
Patience Cryst
Cyrano's Too, Vail, Colorado
Deirdre Davis
deux Cheminées, Philadelphia,
   Pennsylvania
Kay Domurot
Judith Gelzinis Donovan
Double Musky Inn, Girdwood, Alaska
Leslie Dougan
Olivia Erschen
Selma Estrem
Helen Fletcher
Dorothy Gonzales
Barbara Goodman
Lorraine Gooze
Marion Gorman
Bob and Beverly Green
The Greenbrier, White Sulphur Springs,
   West Virginia
Bess Greenstone
Connie Grigsby
Rania Harris
Henry's Family Restaurant,
   Poulsbo, Washington
Rae McIntee Hermens
The Hermitage, Rockingham,
   North Carolina

Mary Hildebrand
Joan Hoien
Jacki Horwitz
Linda Hummel
Roger Jaloux
Liisa Jasinski
Madeleine Kamman
Barbara Karoff
Lynne Kasper
Marlene Kellner
Ouida Kelly
Kennebunk Inn 1799,
   Kennebunk, Maine
Kristine Kidd
Sotiris Kitrilakis
Dona Kuryanowicz
Maria Laudisi
Linda Lee
Lillian Levin
Lion O's Paradise Rock Café, Seattle,
   Washington
Mimmetta LoMonte
L'Orangerie, Los Angeles, California
John Loring
Janine MacGregor
Laurie Magorel
Abby Mandel
Dani Manilla
Linda Marino
Richard McCullough
Michael McLaughlin
Anne Meeker
Miriam Miller
Aline Mobley
Salomon Montezinos
Jefferson Morgan
Jinx Morgan
Janice P. Mulligan
The Newcastle Inn, New Castle,
   Delaware
Donna Nordin
Victoria Nuñez
The Old Milkwagon, Aptos, California
Papa Haydn, Portland, Oregon
Patti's, Grand Rivers, Kentucky
Paulette's, Memphis, Tennessee
Fenella Pearson
Thelma Pressman
Steven Raichlen
Theo Raven
Carolyn Reagan
Richard's Restaurant, Modesto,
   California

Jacky Robert
Jill Roberts
Carol Robertson
Neil Romanoff
Betty Rosbottom
Susan Rosenfeld
Nell Rugee
The Salt Box Restaurant, Ocean City,
   New Jersey
San Ysidro Ranch, Montecito, California
Sarge Oak, Lafayette, Indiana
Jimmy Schmidt
Patricia Scully
Gillian Servais
Edena Sheldon
Nancy Sherman
Janet Showalter
Shirley Slater
Carol Slocum
André Soltner
Leon Soniat
Pam Spano
Lisa Stamm
Bonnie Stern
Stephanie Stokes
Christine Tittel
Doris Tobias
T. K. Tripps, Greensboro,
   North Carolina
Under the Blue Moon, Chestnut Hill,
   Pennsylvania
Jim Van Arsdel
Victoria's, Randolph, Vermont
Vista International
Dorothy Vusich
Elaine Wally
Van Weimer
Whiffletree Inn, Ilion, New York
C. B. White's, Truckee, California
Sheila Wild
Zita Wilensky
Anne Willan
Youngberg's Arcata, California

Additional text was supplied by:
Patricia Connell, *For Perfect Pastry;*
   Hints for Freezing
Marion Gorman, *Whole Wheat Pastry*
Jan Weimer, *Flours for Pastrymaking*

The Knapp Press
is a wholly owned subsidiary of
KNAPP COMMUNICATIONS CORPORATION

Composition by Publisher's Typography

This book is set in Sabon, a face designed by Jan Teischold in 1967 and based on early fonts
engraved by Garamond and Granjon.